W9-BFK-394

ESSENTIAL STOCK PICKING STRATEGIES

ESSENTIAL STOCK PICKING STRATEGIES

What Works on Wall Street

Daniel A. Strachman

John Wiley & Sons, Inc.

Published by John Wiley & Sons, Inc.
Published simultaneously in Canada.

ISBN: 0-471-40063-7

Printed in the United States of America

10 9 8 7 6 5 4 3 2 1

To my parents

The day is short; the task is great.
—Ethics of the Fathers
Chapter II, Verse 20

There's a way to do it better. Find it!
—Thomas A. Edison

CONTENTS

ACKNOWLEDGMENTS

There are many steps and processes that one completes in order to get a book from just an idea to the point where it is bound and sitting on the shelf in a bookstore. All along the way there are many people who contribute to making the concept become a reality. However, a few individuals have contributed greatly to making this particular project happen, and I would like to thank them for their guidance and support during the past year that I have been working on this project. The individuals are in no particular order: Sam Graff, the best newspaperman east of the Mississippi; Sarah Theodore, a fantastic librarian and researcher unlike any other; Desmond MacRae, a truly one-of-a-kind individual with theories on practically everything; and Jeff Zack, a dear friend who always provides me with great advice and guidance on my projects. I need to thank all of the money managers who agreed to be profiled in these pages—because without them there would be no book. Special thanks also to Annette, Stanley, David, Ruth, Amy, and Felice for their guidance and support.

Of course no book would get published without a publisher, so to all of the people at John Wiley & Sons, especially Pamela van Giessen and Joan O'Neil, thanks for everything. I hope this book is everything you intended it to be when you gave me the go-ahead to write it.

DANIEL A. STRACHMAN

New York City
April 2002

INTRODUCTION

Over the past six or seven years everything was the stock market and the stock market was everything. Cabdrivers, teachers, waiters, and window washers—everybody was talking about this stock or that stock and how every single one was going up.

No longer did you need to know anything about fundamental or technical analysis or anything about a company's balance sheet or income statement to make money in the market. All you had to do was place an order, hold it for a day or two, and *bam!* You were a Wall Street whiz!

The stories were all over television, radio, and print, not to mention the Internet. They told of people who made millions when their companies went public or by putting a pittance into a start-up tech company. Some individuals even saw the value of their retirement accounts triple overnight.

Everyone had the bug and the bug had everyone. Even people in other professions got into the act. Investing novices who never before had a penny in the stock market began to expect that they would make 30 to 40 percent a year on their mutual fund investments. And many mutual fund managers and salespeople told them that they were right. It was as if the investing public was under a spell, believing that the market could not go down. The haze of greed blinded everyone.

"I got used to buying a stock at 10 in the morning and making 10 or 15 percent by 2 in the afternoon and selling it before the close," said a graphic designer who lives in Manhattan. "Sometimes it took a day or two, but I would almost always make 20 to 30 percent on every stock I purchased. Trading stocks become a better business than my actual business."

The tech craze seemed to blossom overnight as stocks went from 9 to 90 in a matter of minutes. The demand clearly outweighed the supply. For a while it seemed as if it was never going to end.

Yet as quickly as people started making money, they began to lose it. By the spring of 2000 times had changed—changed for the worse. First the small technology companies began to run out of money (they never made any to begin with) as they burned through the cash they raised by going public. Then the large technology companies started to have problems. Slowly the nontechnology companies fell ill as well, and before you knew it the markets took to their sickbeds and did not seem as if they were ever going to get up.

The problem had too many causes to write about in this book. The stock market from the mid-1990s to early 2000 will be fertile territory for books and business school lectures for years to come. And while many people delight in schadenfreude, I don't, and therefore I have chosen to leave out the horror stories about people losing millions in a month and to move on to the good stuff.

One of the main problems was that for retail investors, trading stocks stopped being fun and turned into something that resembled work.

It stopped being fun because people had to dig to find good investments. Many people—or at least many of those who had experienced such huge growth in their portfolios—had little or no experience picking stocks or making sound investment decisions. These people had grown accustomed to buying anything with a tech or dot-com slant to it without understanding the first thing about the company. Now they came to realize that to invest wisely, you need to understand a company. That takes study, and many people didn't want to put in the time.

The problem wasn't just with the retail investor but also with many of the so-called investment professionals. The tech bug bit them, too, giving them a sort of tech tetanus that left them unable to move out of the sector in time.

Like the rest of the investing public, many of these men and women have also had a hard time picking winners, because the game has changed and they no longer understand the rules. Instead many are sitting in a daze, lost in a new fog.

So what really happened, and how did things get so out of control? Well, I don't really have an answer, nor does anyone else. One thing I do know: If you look at the history of the markets, you will find that markets like the ones of the mid- and late 1990s happen again and again. The difference between the 1990s and other bubbles, though, is the fantastic growth of news and information about the stock market. Many things killed the bull market, but not the least of them was the Internet.

Twenty years ago, it was next to impossible to get market prices in your home or office. Now not only can you get live prices, but you can get indications of who is willing to buy or sell a stock, learn the volume of shares traded, and, in some cases, see who is buying what and why.

"It used to be that the only people who had market information or intelligence were people in the market," said one longtime broker. "Nowadays, everybody not only thinks that they are in the market, but they believe that they have as much information about the market as the professionals have. In some cases they do, but in most cases they don't, and that is why people are getting hurt. Everyone thinks it is a level playing field, but in reality it is not."

When the market did turn into a bear, the media enjoyed reporting that one of the reasons was because very few money managers and day traders had previously experienced a down market. I think they should have reported that those investors and some money managers and day traders had forgotten the past, creating a problem that has stifled the growth of the market. People tend to forget how good they had it and how long it took them to recover from the bad times.

Many people believe that they can predict which way markets and individual stocks will move. Some have been very successful at it, while others have been pretty poor at it. One thing that seems to be certain is that the key to successful investing is being able to withstand both the good times and the bad.

Like the gambler who keeps just enough chips in her pocket to play another day and the soldier who retreats so he can fight again, the key to successful investing is time and the ability to withstand hardship. You have to live to invest another day, and while this may sound easy, it isn't, because we are dealing solely with *money*!

Money—it's been called "a pain in the ass," "the root of all evil," and "the one thing that makes the world go round." Whatever it is, people like it, and they like it even more when it comes to them with ease. They like to spend it, they like to flash it, and some may even like to roll around naked in it.

INTRODUCTION

Many people believe that regardless of who you are, what you do, or how much you have, you can never have enough money.

Back in 1995, I was a trainee working at a large New York institutional brokerage. As part of my training, I rotated through every area of the firm's brokerage units. The trading desks in most firms look the same, so unless someone tells you what a particular desk is trading, it is very hard to distinguish one group from another.

On this particular day, I was in the municipal bond area, an area that was on the verge of extinction, partly because the stock market was on a tear. We were all talking about this new stock issue, Netscape—how it was about to go public and was going to go through the roof, and how we all wanted to short the stock because it seemed unfathomable that the stock of a company that basically did nothing more than make getting to the Internet easier was worth anywhere near the amount it was trading for. Besides, at the time very few people used the Internet for anything more than e-mail.

Little did we know that it was the start of something big!

From that point on, every Internet stock, as well as almost every other initial public offering, seemed to double in price, if not triple, right out of the gate. It was quite a ride. It was a ride that many investors will remember for a very long time. Many will long for the days of the Internet craze—forgetting the heavy losses—and wish for the days of doubles and triples in a matter of hours. They'll look backward nostalgically, of course, only until the market turns and stocks start going up again.

Still, maybe the opportunity exists right now and investors don't see it. Maybe there are people out there who don't need skyrocketing markets or the latest craze to post strong returns. Maybe there are people who have done well and continue to do well regardless of market conditions. This leads me to the idea behind *Essential Stock Picking Strategies: What Works on Wall Street*.

The purpose of this book is to provide you with unique insight into money managers. It is for readers who want to learn about the different investment styles and strategies of money managers who have made sound investment decisions over a significant period of time. It is not to make these men and women out to be the best or necessarily the brightest; it is merely to show that consistency is the most important thing when it comes to investing. The idea is to illustrate that having strict investment principles and following a strict investment strategy is more important then finding the next best thing. I wrote this book to give you a better understanding of what works on Wall Street, so that you can profit from good investment strategies and make money in both bull and bear markets.

I have chosen money managers who have solid track records and who have been in the money management business for some time. Most of them are names that you will not recognize, and there is a reason for that—a reason you will understand when you finish this book.

A great Wall Streeter once said, "Never confuse brains with a bull market." I believe the people profiled in these chapters have the brains to be successful in both bull and bear markets and that these pages offer you the chance to profit from their brains.

ESSENTIAL STOCK PICKING STRATEGIES

★ *chapter one* ★

INVESTING 101

Stocks and the Equity Markets

To understand the money management business, one first has to understand the stock market and how it works.

First one needs to realize that when people say "the stock market" they mean all of the equity markets around the world. And while many of us believe that New York is the center of the universe for everything, many others believe that those of us who think this way are egotistical snobs. When it comes to trading stocks, though, New York is truly the place. Sure, there are other markets around the globe in all the major cities of the world, and there are markets throughout the United States; but everything everywhere having to do with the equity markets gets its cue from the seven square miles that is New York City and the mythical place we all call Wall Street.

In order to understand the stock market and how it works it is important to have a clear understanding of what a stock or equity is (stocks and equities are the exact same thing, and the terms can be used interchangeably). According to the *Dictio-*

nary of Business Terms, there are two types of stock: common and preferred.

> **Common stock** security representing an ownership interest in a corporation. Ownership may also be shared with preferred stock, which has prior claim on any dividends to be paid and, in the event of liquidation, to the distribution of the corporation's assets. As owners of the corporation, common stockholders assume the primary risk if business is poor, realize the greater return in the event of success, and elect the board of directors that controls the company.[1]
>
> **Preferred stock** part of the capital stock of a corporation that enjoys priority over the remaining stock, or common stock, in the distribution of dividends and in the event of dissolution of the corporation, also in the distribution of assets.[2]

Now let's explore the markets and how they work.

Brokers have been trading stocks in the United States since the 1700s. However, organized buying and selling of stocks started at the foot of Manhattan near Wall Street and are shrouded in scandal. According to Charles Geisst, a leading Wall Street historian, there were few if any formal rules or regulations governing the trading of stocks until speculator William Duer caused a financial meltdown. Duer, a British expatriate, was a land speculator who borrowed large amounts of money from banks. He overextended himself and could not pay off his debts, causing some banks to fail and others to become very nervous that a landslide effect would hurt their balance sheets and in turn cause the nation's financial system to completely collapse.

The failures and potential failures of the banks were the stimulus for 24 brokers to meet under a buttonwood tree in 1792 and sign the famed Buttonwood Agreement, which formalized trading. This formalization provided an outlet or arena for institutions, both financial and nonfinancial, to issue stock and in turn raise capital to not only expand their businesses but also make the businesses stronger and avoid the risk of collapse due to one individual's recklessness.

Duer had a different fate. He was sent to debtors' prison, where he died penniless.[3]

Today one can still see the spot where the agreement was signed. Although the buttonwood tree is long gone, the location is part of the office complex at 60 Wall Street that is home to a number of Wall Street's most powerful firms, including JP Morgan Chase.

Trading continued for a time outside by the tree. In 1793 a group of traders decided to move indoors, a move that in 1817 evolved into the New York Stock and Exchange Board. Another group of traders continued to trade outside by the curb; however, this group eventually went inside as well, forming what is now the American Stock Exchange (AMEX).

In 1863 the New York Stock and Exchange Board changed its name to its current *nom de plume*: the New York Stock Exchange. The NYSE established formalized hours for trading in 1873: 10 A.M. to 3 P.M. weekdays and 10 A.M. to noon on Saturday (prior to that the hours had been flexible). Since 1873, the New York Stock Exchange has changed its hours of operation just three times—in 1887, 1974, and 1985. The change in 1985 moved the trading day from the hours of 10 A.M. to 4 P.M. to its current hours, 9:30 A.M. to 4 P.M.

The curb traders moved inside in 1921 as the New York Curb Market Association (later the New York Curb Exchange).

In 1953 the Curb Exchange changed its name to the American Stock Exchange and in 1998 the American Stock Exchange merged with the Nasdaq Stock Market. The New York Stock Exchange continues to remain an independent entity owned by its seat holders.

The Nasdaq Stock Market was born in 1971 as a result of the Securities and Exchange Commission's decision that the over-the-counter securities industry needed to be automated. The SEC asked the National Association of Securities Dealers, Inc. to develop a market for these securities. This action created the first electronic stock market.

These three—the New York Stock Exchange, the American Stock Exchange, and the Nasdaq Stock Market—are the primary markets where stocks are traded. While regional and other electronic markets operate and have for some time, for the most part stock trades are executed on the NYSE, the AMEX, or the Nasdaq. There are many places to learn about the evolution of the stock markets and how they work, and, as with most subjects these days, the best place to start is the Internet.

The NYSE and AMEX differ from the Nasdaq in one significant respect. The New York and American exchanges are both called a "specialist market," and the Nasdaq is a "dealer market."

The difference is in the way orders are taken and executed. A specialist market—also known as an agency auction market system—is designed to allow the public to meet the public as much as possible, meaning people trade with each other and do not work with dealers. Simply put, it is a place where buyers and sellers meet face-to-face to trade their stocks. The majority of volume in these markets occurs with no intervention from dealers or specialists.

The specialists make markets in stocks and work on the floors of the NYSE and the AMEX. The responsibility of specialists is to make fair and orderly markets in the stocks that are assigned to them. They must always yield to public orders, which means that they may not trade for their own accounts when there are public bids and offers. While the lay public is never allowed to actually enter to floor of the exchanges to trade, the "public" in this case is the brokers who act on behalf of firms and the traders who act on behalf of themselves.

The specialists' job is to eliminate imbalances of supply and demand when they occur and maintain a narrow spread in the market for each stock. The specialists are governed by the exchange, which has in place strict guidelines for trading and continuity that must be observed. Regardless of market conditions, specialists are required to make a continuous market in their stocks. After the crash of 1987, many of the smaller specialist firms were forced to merge with larger firms or went out of business because of that rule. As long as someone was willing to sell stock, they had to buy it regardless of price and even if no one else wanted it. This caused a drain on their capital and in turn forced them to either take the action of merging with some firm that had a stronger balance sheet or go out of business.

The Nasdaq is also commonly, and somewhat confusingly, called the OTC or over-the-counter market. The Nasdaq market is an interdealer market represented by over 420 registered securities dealers trading more than 4,750 different issues.[4] These dealers are called market makers.

Unlike on the NYSE or AMEX, the Nasdaq market does not operate as an auction market. Instead, market makers are expected to compete against each other to post the best quotes (best bid/ask prices) on the system for all buyers and sellers to see. The Nasdaq does not have a trading floor like the NYSE and AMEX; instead the market is operated through a series of computer terminals that dealers and traders access electronically. However, as the excitement around the stock market grew in the mid-1990s and the bull market charged on, the Nasdaq opened a center called the Nasdaq MarketSite in the heart of Times Square in New York City to provide the public with some view of its operation.

Investors are able to access information through the Nasdaq Quotation Dissemination Services, which shows all the bid offers, ask offers, size of each offer (size of the market), and the market makers making the offers in real time. The size of the market is simply the number of shares the market maker is prepared to buy or sell at a specific price.

A market maker, like a specialist, is required to make a two-sided market every day. The brokerage firm can handle customer orders either as a broker or as a dealer/principal. When the brokerage firm acts as a broker, it simply arranges the trade between buyer and seller, and charges a commission for its services. When the brokerage firm acts as a dealer/principal, it's either buying or selling from its own account (to or from the customer) or in turn acting as a market maker.

The customer is charged either a markup or a markdown, depending on whether the customer is buying or selling. The brokerage firm can never charge both a markup (or markdown) and a commission. Whether acting as a broker or as a dealer/principal, the brokerage firm is required to disclose its role in the transaction to the customer.

In the OTC market, the public almost always executes an order with a dealer, which means it is nearly impossible to buy on the bid or sell on the ask. The dealers can buy on the bid even though the public is bidding. Despite the requirement of making a market, in the case of market makers, unlike specialists, there is no one firm that has to take responsibility if trading is not fair or orderly or that has to offer to buy the stock when it begins to drop in price.

Many believe that during the crash of 1987 the NYSE performed much better than the Nasdaq. This was in spite of the fact that some stocks had more than 30 market makers making a market in them. Many OTC firms simply stopped making markets or answering phones until the crash was over and the dust settled, allowing the public to lose out while they sat on the sidelines.

There is quite a significant amount of academic research that has shown an auction market such as the NYSE results in better trades (in tighter ranges, creating less volatility, and with less difference in price between trades). One would think, when comparing the multiple market makers on the Nasdaq with the few specialists on the NYSE and AMEX, that this would not be the case, but research has shown it to be true. However, now that all of the markets have moved away from trading in fractions and have begun trading in decimals, the research may be somewhat skewed and outdated.

For the most part when people talk about the stock market they talk about the Dow or the S&P or the Nasdaq. Each of these refers to an index that tracks a specific group of stocks that are thought to be representative of the market as a whole.

The Dow Jones Industrial Average is by far the most commonly known and is accepted around the world by most of the public as the pulse of Wall Street. If the Dow is up, things must be good; if it is down, things must be bad. However, the Dow is only a small representation of the total stock market in that it consists of just 30 companies. Started in 1896 as a tool to measure daily stock market performance of nonrailroad stocks, the index initially tracked 12 stocks; by 1916 it tracked 20, and by 1928 it had grown to its current number of 30. Of the original 12 companies that comprised the Dow from its first days only General Electric is still around. Since the beginning the Dow has been computed daily, first by Charles Dow himself and then by others in his organization.

Similar to the Dow, the Standard & Poor's 500 was started by a leading financial information company. Initially the index included just 233 stocks. Because of its size it was difficult to compute, so the company calculated and published it once a week. By 1957 the index had grown to its current size, 500 of the largest publicly traded companies.

While the New York Stock Exchange and the American Stock Exchange have indexes that track stocks that trade on their floors, the Nasdaq index is a much more thought after measure of the strength of the market. The Nasdaq index, launched in 1985, is made up of the 100 largest nonfinancial U.S. and non-U.S. companies listed on the Nasdaq National Market. In the five-year period that ended in December 2000, the index rose over 1,670 percent, compared to 597 percent for the Dow and 525 percent for the S&P. The Nasdaq casts a very wide net when it comes to providing companies with a place for their stocks to trade. Because of the mammoth size and scope of the market, many of the most important and least important companies trade through its web of computers.

Investment Basics

The proliferation of the Internet has caused markets around the world to become more transparent. Up-to-the-minute market data can literally be accessed almost instantaneously with the click of a mouse or the stroke of a keyboard. The idea that both large and small, retail and institutional investors can access the same financial news at the same time has truly leveled the playing field for investing. Ten years ago, the person who got the best information first had an advantage over everyone else. Now, because news and information are broadcast so widely and so quickly, it is not the person who gets it first but rather the person who acts on it in the smartest way who has the advantage.

This leads us to the people profiled in these pages. As mentioned earlier, almost everyone thinks they can pick stocks and manage money. They believe that because of the Internet they have the same information as everyone else, they are as smart as if not smarter than everyone else, and therefore they should have the ability to be as successful at investing as the professionals. The problem is that they don't have the skills, are not as smart, and really have no business being in the market or managing money.

It is crazy to think that you can read a book, scan some magazines, look at a few websites, or talk to a friend and then be able to pick stocks. I believe that picking stocks and managing money is about as difficult as operating on a patient or designing an office building. Unfortunately, most people disagree with me on this and instead expect that if they are good at a few things they will also be good at managing money and picking stocks.

This, in my opinion, is rather egotistical and quite a bit of nonsense. What they are saying is that professional money managers and financial planners do not have any special skills to make them more or less qualified at managing money.

I believe, however, that you can truly be successful at only one or two things. If you want to manage money successfully you have to be committed to it just like any other profession.

Surgeons are good surgeons because they went to school and they practice, and the same can be said for money managers.

Managing money needs to be taken seriously, and the only way to do so is to focus on it and it solely as a doctor does surgery. And just like some surgeons are better than others, I believe some money managers are better than others.

Therefore, I have chosen people to profile in this book who I believe are a step above most. These are not the best money managers on the face of the earth, nor are they going to be right every time. But they do seem to know what they are doing, and, as they say, the numbers never lie.

The key to successfully managing money is the ability to stick to one's investment guidelines or plan. You have to know what you are doing, why you are doing it, and how you are going to react to every situation that could possibly occur.

Peter Lynch, the famed money manager from Fidelity Investments, once said that Americans spend more time picking out the colors of their refrigerators than they do picking stocks or thinking about managing their money. (Perhaps this is because you look at the refrigerator every time you want a cold drink or something to eat, and you look at your portfolio only monthly or quarterly when the statement comes.

You need to find a professional who has a plan and knows how to execute it, stick to it, and, most importantly, be successful at it. Like most plans, occasionally it will need tweaking, but a good planner understands this and can adapt the plan accordingly.

Mutual Funds and Hedge Funds

The most common way of investing is through a mutual fund. Mutual funds have been around since the early 1900s and over the past 20 years have grown considerably. Today there are more mutual funds than there are individual stocks.

The basic concept behind the mutual fund is that for a relatively small cost it offers a place for people to invest their money with a professional organization that will manage the money more effectively than they can on their own.

There are basically two types of mutual funds, load and no-load. Load funds charge investors a fee—usually up front—which is basically the commission for the broker who told the investor about the fund, while the other part of the fee goes to the money management firm or the fund complex. No-load funds do not charge an up-front commission; they charge a management fee and a marketing fee. Some people believe that a load fund is better than a no-load fund because investors are getting more professional managers or a stronger organization with greater investment advice, while a no-load fund comes with little or no advice from the broker. In my opinion it really does not matter. For the most part all mutual fund managers are interested in being successful by beating their benchmarks and I don't think one type of fund is better than the other. The key is finding the right fund or funds to meet your investment needs and wants; sometimes it is easier to do with a broker than it is on your own.

However, in a load fund that has multiple classes of shares such as A, B, or C shares, I would always buy the A shares. Even though you have to pay an up-front charge for A shares, it is better to get the fees out of the way in the beginning than pay them later. If you look at the cost associated with buying and owning the A shares versus the B or C shares over the same period, you will find that it ends up costing you less to own the A shares with the up-front fees than the Bs or Cs, with the backend fees.

Mutual funds are basically for the masses; you can see their prices daily in the newspaper or on the World Wide Web. They offer a great deal of liquidity, meaning you can get in and out of the investment with ease; and because there are so many of them out there, it is relatively easy to find a fund or group of funds that fits your needs.

Another type of investment is the hedge fund. Hedge funds were started in the late 1940s by a man named Alfred Winslow Jones. Jones was a sociologist/journalist who basically got fed up writing about Wall Street and decided to participate in it. Jones believed he was as smart as the people he was writing about and that he, too, could be successful at managing money and in turn provide a good life for his family.

A hedge fund is nothing more than a private investment vehicle that is open to a limited number of accredited investors and institutions and that is unregulated by the Securities and Exchange Commission. Mutual funds are heavily regulated by the SEC and therefore can accept an unlimited number of investors regardless of their investment experience or expertise. While some think that this is where the differences end, it is not the case. One of the key differences between hedge funds and mutual funds is leverage.

Hedge funds, by definition, focus on hedging the portfolio. This means that they construct a portfolio that is able to perform well in up markets and not as badly as others in down markets. The idea is that in both cases the hedge fund will outperform the benchmarks—be up more than the benchmark in a good market and be down less than the benchmark in a bad market.

The differences do not end there, however; another key difference is fees. Mutual fund complexes charge loads/commissions, a management fee, and a marketing or 12b-1 fee. Hedge funds charge management fees and an incentive fee. The management fee is usually 1 percent of the total assets under management. An incentive fee is nothing more than a fee based on the performance of the portfolio. In most cases the incentive fee is 20 percent of the profits—for every dollar in profit the hedge fund earns, the manager will keep 20 cents. Some people believe the fees are egregious and downright criminal—as described by *Forbes* magazine in a scathing article in its August 6, 2001 issue about hedge fund fees, managers, and the overall industry. The article, titled "The $500 Billion Hedge Fund Folly," said that many of the people in the hedge fund industry were nothing more than "race track touts" and that fees were "outrageous."[5]

Whether the article was correct or not is basically a toss-up. It did make some interesting points about some of the bad apples, if you will, in the hedge fund business, but when it comes to the fee structure it left one thing out: Investors don't seem to mind the prices they are paying for the goods they are receiving. It seems that as long as the strategies are working and the returns continue to come in, investors will not mind paying the fees. However, when things go south investors may have questions and wonder what they are paying for and why the price is so high.

Fees and structure aside, the most important difference between mutual funds and hedge funds is what I call the "skin in the game" aspect of the product. The "skin in the game" aspect simply refers to the fact that most hedge fund managers have most if not all of their liquid net worth invested in their own hedge funds. This means that when the funds do well they don't simply earn fees, they also see their investments grow; similarly, when the funds do poorly they lose not only fees but also their own investments.

"If I did not have any of my money in the fund, how could I

ask investors for theirs?" inquired Paul Wong, manager of Edgehill Capital in Greenwich, Connecticut. "If I don't believe in myself, I can't expect anyone else to, and therefore I'd have no right being in this business."

This is a very important point. Most mutual fund managers have little of their own net worth tied up in their funds, which makes very little sense; it is like the auto mechanic going to another repair shop when his car breaks down or the chef choosing to eat at another restaurant. Money managers need to have "skin in the game." If they don't, you shouldn't, either.

Another difference between mutual funds and hedge funds is that hedge funds are not easily understood by or portrayed favorably in the press. There is very little public information about hedge funds available, unlike mutual funds, and hedge funds are not allowed to advertise or for the most part talk about what they are or are not doing in the market at a given time.

There are occasions when hedge fund managers do discuss investment style and strategy and can be found doing so on the business broadcast networks or in the press, but generally the industry as a whole is quite tight-lipped and often appears to operate quite secretively. The reason for this secrecy is not because managers want to appear better than everyone else or that they want to keep up a veil of mystery about their styles and strategies; it is because if the SEC or IRS suspects them of advertising, they can get into an awful lot of trouble.

"It does not make any sense whatsoever for me to go on TV or be interviewed in the paper," said a hedge fund manager who requested anonymity. "All I need is for the SEC or IRS to construe what I am saying is advertising or public marketing, and I will have more legal problems than I will know what to do with. I much prefer to keep to myself and earn my living by managing the portfolio and attracting investors through word of mouth."

Mutual funds are quite the opposite. Give a manager a time or place to speak and for the most part he or she will be there. One of the reasons for this is because there is a great amount of competition among mutual fund complexes for assets. And while there seems to be an infinite amount of assets available—in the summer of 2001 many believed there was close to a trillion dollars sitting on the sidelines in passbook savings accounts, money markets, or certificates of deposit waiting for the market to turn—fund complexes were and are constantly lining up to chase those assets. The more a manager is exposed to television viewers, in the newspapers, and in front of audiences, the more likely the fund will attract assets. For this reason the media is literally littered with mutual fund managers who have something to say or at least think they do.

The third most important difference between mutual funds and hedge funds is the ability to go short. While some mutual funds have the ability to go short, for the most part it is not a money management strategy that is practiced often by the masses. Going short is not only counterintuitive to most people's way of thinking, it is also not an easy thing to do. Some people have called it just plain un-American, while others call it quite profitable.

The basic idea behind shorting a stock is that the investor is betting that the company is going to fail and therefore the stock is going to decrease in value instead of increase. The short seller borrows the securities from a brokerage firm; sells them into the market at the price of, say, $30 per share; waits for the stock to fall in price eventually to anything less than $30 and the transaction cost; and then buys the shares back and replaces the ones borrowed. The profit is spread between the sale price, in this case $30, and the buyback price plus transaction costs.

Shorting stocks is something that many have a hard time doing successfully. Besides finding the right stock to sell short, you also need to deal with the mechanics of the trade, which is not always so easy, either. I know of one mutual fund manager who was considered by most to be one of the best information technology managers around, and yet when it came to finding stocks to short he was basically incapable of doing it. All the money he made on the upside was wiped out by the stocks he thought were going to decrease in value on the downside.

Shorting successfully is a skill that many have tried and few have mastered. It is not that hedge fund managers are simply better at picking losers and winners than mutual fund managers are; it is just that it is a skill and a mind-set that some would say is crucial to success in the hedge fund industry.

Unfortunately, many mutual fund managers believe that they can be successful at shorting, when in actuality they have no real understanding of how the short should and will work and why it should or should not be successful before they put the position on.

"Shorting is very hard. It is counterintuitive to everything you think you need to be doing in order to be a successful money manager," said a hedge fund manager. "It is a very difficult decision to make. It often takes me twice if not three times as long to make a decision to short a stock than it does to make a decision to put on a long position."

While some say shorting is an art form that many portfolio managers strive to achieve mastery over, others simply are thankful that according to their mutual fund's prospectus they are not allowed to do it.

"If the chief investment officer of my firm told me that we needed to start including shorts in the portfolio, I would do it but probably would not be very good at it," said a manager who manages two mutual funds for a small fund complex in New York. "It is much easier for me to hedge the portfolio with options on noncorrelated stocks than it is to find stocks that I think will decrease in price."

While most portfolio managers have a considerable amount of schooling and experience as either an assistant portfolio manager or a research analyst, some have little or no formal market education. It seems that no matter how strong a background you have and no matter what credentials you carry, guts are what is important.

Many of the managers I have spoken to over the past year or so have said that the hardest part of the job is sticking with their convictions.

"In these types of markets it is very hard to make investment decisions because there is so much volatility and market uncertainty," said a portfolio manager. "It is even harder, however, to stick with a decision once I make it and the stock starts moving the other way. You really need to have a lot of conviction and determination as well as a belief that what you are doing is right. You can't sit around and second-guess yourself, because if you do the portfolio will never be successful."

I am pretty sure Guts 101 is not a class that is taught at any of the business schools on the East Coast, but maybe it is on the West Coast. Besides lacking classes in guts, many of the top business schools do not even teach courses in portfolio management. From a number of discussions with deans at two of New York's most prestigious schools I learned that neither offers a basic portfolio management course.

"We don't really offer a class in how to manage money or buy and sell securities," said Michael Keenen, assistant dean of the finance department at New York University's Stern School of Business. "Sure, there are classes students can take on the finance side of investment theory, but when it comes down to money management there really is nothing."

Keenen said one reason for the lack of interest on the part of the schools to offer courses on investment styles and strategies is because very few of the styles and strategies actually beat the indexes.

"The academic world is not interested in promoting theories or practices that cannot beat a computer-generated random index of securities," he said. "We are annoyed that nothing more than some basic portfolio modeling seems to be needed to outperform the market."

Warren Buffett and Charlie Munger

However, do not tell that to Warren Buffett or Charlie Munger. Buffett I am sure you all have heard about, while Munger a few of you have as well. For the benefit of those who do not recognize Munger's name I suggest that you read on; for those who do, please skip the next few pages.

Buffett, as we all know, is considered by most to be one of the greatest investors of all time. He is a strict believer in the value investing theories of Graham and Dodd[6] and for the past 30-odd years has had a very successful track record finding solid companies to invest in through his vehicle Berkshire Hathaway, headquartered in Omaha, Nebraska.

Charlie Munger is Buffett's partner; he lives in Los Angeles but is an integral part of the Berkshire machine that has seen its stock price grow at an annual rate of about 27 percent for the past 36 years. Buffett himself credits Munger with converting Buffett from a strict old-fashioned Graham value investor to the ultimate buy-and-hold value strategist.[7]

"Charlie shoved me in the direction of not just buying bargains as Ben Graham had taught me," Buffett said in a *Forbes* piece. "This was the real impact he had on me. It took a powerful force to move me from Graham's limiting views. It was the power of Charlie's mind. He expanded my horizon."[8]

Munger, who was 78 at the time of this writing, was born and raised in Omaha; he left Nebraska to attend the University of Michigan. After a few semesters he transferred to the California Institute of Technology, but dropped out of Caltech without earning a degree. Upon his return from serving as a meteorological officer in Air Force during World War II, he entered Harvard without an undergraduate degree and graduated with a law degree in 1948. Munger then left Massachusetts for California, where he began his law career. He continued practicing law, setting up his own firm, Munger, Tolles, Olson, and also began a small money management firm that he operated from an office in the Pacific Stock Exchange.

In the late 1970s Buffett and Munger started working together as a result of two of Munger's holdings being merged into Berkshire Hathaway. Since 1978 he has served as vice chairman of Berkshire, and he is also active in a number of the Berkshire portfolio companies where he serves on boards of directors and provides advisory services.

What has made the company so unique is that while many believe and operate under the perception that the pair's success is based on picking stocks, the truth is that the success is based on their ability to pick companies.

While Buffett and Munger are renowned as stock pickers, they have long preferred to have Berkshire grow not by buying stocks that go up but by adding businesses, wrote Carol Loomis in *Fortune* magazine in February 2001.[9] The article, in which Loomis admitted her friendship with Buffett, was a little too feel-good for my taste, but it did provide a unique look at the company's moves during the previous year. One has to question its bias, however, when the author of the article admits in the beginning of the piece that she edits the company's annual report.

However, Loomis did provide some insight into how Berkshire operates and the firm's ideas behind its purchases. She wrote that Buffett prefers dealing with managers of real working business and providing them with opportunity to help them grow by building on their accomplishments. Once Berkshire acquires a company, Buffett and Munger pretty much leave the company to its existing management and let them continue to manage the business. Loomis wrote that during a meeting with the directors of a recently acquired company Buffett gave a directive familiar to many of his companies: "Just keep on doing what you're doing. We're never going to tell a .400 hitter how to change his batting stance."[10]

Value investing dates as far back as people can remember, for everyone always has looked and always will continue to look for a good buy. However, it really came into play in the 1940s and 1950s after publication of the book *Security Analysis* by Benjamin Graham and David L. Dodd. The book itself continues to be a top seller around the world and is the basis for almost everyone's investment style and strategies. Its strength lies in the fact that today, over 65 years since it was first published, its pages still offer "practical utility." Many believe that no other book provides information on how to look at a company's past performance and determine how it may do in the future.

In a review of the latest edition of the book, in the *Wall Street Journal* in 1996, Roger Lowenstein, a leading Wall Street author and then staff writer at the *Journal*, wrote that his only complaint about the book was that its publisher,

McGraw-Hill, had put too steep a price tag on the book and produced too small an edition.[11]

Whether an investor has read it or not, somewhere, somehow, someone the investor has gotten investment or money management advice from has learned something from the book. If you have not read it, I suggest that you do. Graham and Dodd provide unique insight into how to value securities and how to make investment decisions based on those valuations and analyses.

So what does it all mean? It seems the main thing for Buffett and Munger is finding value, for the specialist on the floor of the stock exchange it is to ensure an orderly market, for the market maker it is to make sure not to get caught between the bid and the ask, and for you it means basically that investing is hard work. It is a job. It is something that should not be taken lightly, and it is something that demands great skill and understanding in order to be successful. Hopefully, by the time you finish reading this book you will have accomplished the following three goals.

The Due Diligence Process

First, you will have a better understanding of how professional money managers (in this group I include hedge fund mangers, mutual fund managers, and pension fund managers) make investment decisions and operate on a day-to-day basis.

Second, you will understand growth investing, sector investing, value investing, momentum investing, and macro investing and how each of the strategies is different and yet all are somewhat intertwined.

And third, you will have acquired a continued thirst for investment knowledge. No one book is the be all and end all of any one topic. To truly understand how things work it takes time, patience, and most important, a willingness to learn. I don't expect anyone to finish this book and say, "Okay, that's enough—I am done. I can now pick investment managers, and I can even *be* an investment manager!" This book should make you think; it should make you better prepared to ask questions and understand the answers.

The following short digression explains why asking questions that on the surface appear to have little or no relevance can actually turn out to be very important.

Once a manager of a now-defunct global macro hedge fund and I were discussing investor due diligence. He found it interesting to meet with potential investors and explain to them what the fund's strategy was and how he and his team managed its assets. What he found even more fun, however, were the questions that he got from potential investors. He often found that investors that he thought would have little or no investment knowledge knew more about the strategy than he did, and those whom he expected to have considerable knowledge had none.

The best question he ever heard from a potential investor was, "Can I have your wife's phone number?" The manager asked the potential investor why, and she explained, "Before I can invest a dime in your fund, I want to know how you act when you are away from the office, and the best person to get that information from is your wife."

The manager became quite anxious; he was not necessarily as interested in the investor's money as he was in his wife's response to the potential investor's questions. He provided her with the phone number, and eventually she decided to invest some money in the fund.

"She wanted to know how I react when something happens

that is beyond my control," he said. "My wife told her that in most cases I am calm, cool, and collected. She did tell her that sometimes I lose it, and her response was, 'Everybody does. The question is, how bad does he get.' "

The manager to this day calls this investor Attila the Hun. The moral of the story is that everything is related.

Remember one last thing: No matter how much advice, guidance, or support you have, you will never, ever be able to determine which way the market will go. It is totally uncontrollable. It acts on its own without regard to you, your feelings, your needs, or your wants. The key is to understand that it is beyond your control and act accordingly. You need to have a plan, a plan that you stick with regardless of market movements, your feelings, or outside pressures.

And now let's move on to explore essential stock picking strategies.

★ *chapter two* ★

GROWTH AND VALUE MANAGERS

In the spring of 2001, while I was researching this book, I read an article that said that before you invest a single dime in stocks, bonds, or what have you, you need to ask one simple question: "What am I looking for from my money?" Or, put another way, what are my goals and objectives?[1]

The article seemed to be dead on and the question so simple and straightforward that it could be used, by replacing the word "money," for life issues, career questions, and more. It provides a tool to find the answers as well as the guidance to make important decisions with just a few small words.

Still, most investors do not ask themselves that question when it comes to picking stocks for their portfolios or investing in mutual funds. Instead, they are caught up in the moment and end up getting burned.

Long gone are the days of buying a stock at 10 A.M. and having it go up 20 percent by 2:30 P.M. Investors need to do their homework and not be lazy. Before they get to the point of buying, they need to understand why they are investing, what their goal is, how much risk they are willing to take, and how much time they have.

With the market falling, the Internet bubble bursting, and things getting out of control in terms of losses and lost opportunities, many investment pros have started to give advice about how to construct a diversified portfolio and how to make investments that can do well in bad markets as well as good.

One of the most interesting bits of information came from a report issued by Morningstar, Inc.: "If your mutual fund had an experienced manager, there's a better than 50–50 chance you felt less pain than the average domestic stock fund investor during the recent market dips."[2]

The Chicago-based mutual fund tracking company studied all the funds in its database that managed more than $100 million. On average, funds with managers or management teams with at least four years' experience lost less money in the year between March 2000 and March 2001 than either the S&P 500 or the average domestic stock mutual fund.

"Though a resurgence in value funds during the 12-month period [of the study] helped the experienced managers look good, because many tenured fund managers lean toward the value end of the spectrum, funds with seasoned hands tended to do well in all respective categories," said Daniel Culloton, managing editor of the Morningstar news team, in a press release. "There's evidence that veterans of both value and growth investing camps added an advantage."

The Morningstar study went on to say, however, that because no two markets are the same, it is unclear how the funds would perform should the market either continue to decline or reverse itself.

Yet I am personally betting on experienced mangers versus novice managers to guide my investments throughout these turbulent times, and I think you should, too. The following profiles should provide you with great insight into value and growth investing in small-, mid-, and large-cap stocks across the entire market.

The goal of this chapter is to provide you with information on how to make a decision on where the bulk of your assets should go in your quest for building a diversified portfolio. Remember, it is important to have a portfolio that takes advantage of various money management styles and strategies. Each of the following managers represents unique strategies focused on growth and value.

Warren Isabelle

While most investors were shell-shocked at the sight of their portfolios after the market's decline throughout 2000 and 2001, investors in the ICM/Isabelle Small Cap Value fund were thankful.

"The goal of the fund is to produce an investment vehicle that can weather all of the market's storms," said Isabelle. "One of the things that has helped us is that the area of the market that we cover hasn't really been in mind lately."

Throughout the 1990s bull market, small company stocks did well. Still, they did not keep pace with big companies that seemed to attract all the money going into the market and most of the performance, as well.

"Everything that had been driving the bull market was big companies. Names like Cisco, EMC, and Intel were behind the performance," Isabelle said. "So it is not surprising that it was very easy for seasoned and not-so-seasoned investors to gravitate to those companies."

Isabelle got involved in the stock market in the 1970s when he saw a Merrill Lynch pamphlet on how to read a financial statement and how the stock market works.

"Many people tell you that they started off with nothing or no money, but I truly had no money," he said. "I had just flunked out of Worcester Polytechnic Institute because of problems at home and was working as the office manager at a local company that made oil storage tanks."

On his birthday in 1975 he was laid off and decided to go back to school. He entered the Technological Institute at the University of Massachusetts in Lowell, completed his undergraduate work, and then enrolled in the University of Massachusetts for a master's in polymer science and engineering. Upon completing his master's, he entered into a Ph.D. program.

"I was in a Ph.D. program that I hated, the publish or perish thing, and so I left and went to Wharton to get an MBA," he said. "Just when everyone thought I was safe and could get into a mainstream career, I went to work with dairy farmers in California."

His wife's cousin's husband ran a dairy farm, and although he had a lot of vision, he couldn't make his ideas work. Isabelle went there, first, to bring the finance side of the business into the twentieth century; next, to provide more sophisticated liaison with the farm's credit sources; and third, to use his scientific background to find ways to make the business more efficient.

"At the time, the price of milk in California was state-regulated by district. They would take the average costs, so basically the government decided how much we could sell our milk for," he said. "We would get paid by the cooperatives like clockwork, so the key was to control our costs. What we did was find alternative nutrition sources for the cows, so that instead of feeding them with high-cost grain we would use other types of food."

Isabelle set up an alternative food-source business that took advantage of the many local farm cooperatives, including those that sold to the wine maker Gallo and tomato processor Contadina.

"I used to go to local cooperatives and basically take their garbage—the pumice—left over from the processing of the grapes and tomatoes, put it into huge pits, pump the water out of it, put it through a centrifuge, and drain out the protein. I was able to feed that to the cows at a cheaper cost than buying grain," he said. "The problem was things got so good that the two partners fought and I basically left because it was no longer working."

Even while he was experiencing life on the dairy farm, he found time to invest in the market. Along with some of the people he was working with in California, he started buying stocks in companies like General Dynamics Corporation and Boeing Company.

"I am living in an apartment complex and I start seeing that the place is beginning to fill up, and eventually there are no vacancies," he said. "I knew all these kids weren't coming out there to be dairy farmers, so I started talking to them. I found out that most of them were engineers from Ohio State and the University of Michigan, and they were going to work for General Dynamics, Boeing, and Litton Industries, Inc. I knew something was going on, and it was that Reagan had started the defense boom and the contractors were ramping up their operations."

When Isabelle left California and came back to Massachusetts in 1982, the Dow Jones Industrial Average was in the mid-700s. He took a job as a junior analyst at the Hartford Financial Services Group, Inc., and gave up on the dairy business.

He spent a year at the Hartford and realized rather quickly that it was not the place for him to make a career. He found his next job in Boston, through an advertisement in the *Wall Street Journal*.

"I saw an ad in the paper that the Pioneer Group was looking for a chemical analyst. I sent them a resume, figuring I would never hear from them, but after about six interviews, I got the job," he said. "At the time, they came to me and said, 'Look, we have $600 million in chemicals. They are yours. Tell us what to do with them.'"

Today Isabelle uses the same model to pick stocks that he used at Pioneer, something he calls "real economics."

"The best and easiest way to describe real economics is through cash flows, because, let's face it, all businesses are conducted through cash. At the end of the day you want cash," he said. "If you can't get cash out, then stock is not worth anything, so you have to figure that if you put cash in, you want to earn a return on the cash."

Unlike some other managers, Isabelle looks at a company for its economic value and from there puts it through a modeling process to determine whether it should go into his portfolio.

"When I started out covering chemicals, I decided that I was also going to cover any company that was remotely connected to the chemical industry," he said. "So we started out with the regular chemical companies; then we went to the materials companies, cosmetics, and conglomerates; and before you knew it, I had all sorts of things, which helped me out."

But what really helped him out and put him on the map, both at Pioneer and with other Boston mutual fund companies, was the rash of mergers that hit the chemical industry in the late 1980s. At the time Pioneer had significant positions in some of the merging companies, and people started paying attention to Isabelle's stock picking skills.

"It was not like today, where you are an analyst for six months and then they tell you, 'Go and run a portfolio,'" he said. "In those days you had to get seasoned somewhat before they would let you manage money. Because I had picked some good stocks and had some seasoning, they decided to let me become a portfolio manager."

His first stint as portfolio manager was running a $400 million small-cap sleeve of the Pioneer 2 fund, at the time the firm's largest, with $4 billion in assets.

"When I started out as an analyst, I focused on the large companies like Monsanto and DuPont, but I got a reputation over time for doing really well with small companies," he said.

In 1990, Pioneer decided to introduce a growth trust, a series trust with three funds: a gold fund, an equity income fund, and an aggressive value fund.

"I have always been one to get my proper baptism. Well, as soon as I started managing the growth trust, not two weeks later, the Kuwaiti war started and the fund went from a per-share net asset value of $10 to $7, and people started to look at me as if I had two heads," he said. "I was preaching small cap because every piece of evidence I had showed that the area was horribly undervalued and at an all-time low."

Two heads or not, things were pretty bad. While some of the investors may have been assembling the gallows up in Salem for him, in October the market turned, and turned with a vengeance. Isabelle stuck with his portfolio throughout the decline, so when things started to happen, it was positioned to take advantage of the turn.

"I went around to all the analysts at Pioneer and asked them for two of their best small-cap ideas and I put them in the portfolio," he said. "The key for me was that I was able to stick to my guns. I think that there is nothing more important than sticking with what you believe in. If you have conviction, you have to let the crap flow through but your cream will always rise to the top."

Over time the portfolio continued to grow and Isabelle was given more responsibility at Pioneer, where in addition to being a portfolio manager he became director of research. Eventually he realized the fund was getting too big and that the best thing to do was to cap its assets. For Pioneer, though, the fund was the only one that was selling. The company decided to keep the fund open and to launch a new small-cap fund. The new fund took off like a rocket and within seven months went from zero to over $500 million in assets. Then the company closed the fund to new investors.

At this point, Isabelle was running three funds as well as being director of research and head of the firm's special equities unit. The fund company was at the height of its growth, bringing in on average $200 million in new assets every month.

"The problem was that there was too much going on, and I needed to get back to being focused on managing money and lose some of the responsibilities that they had given me," he said. "They had sort of put together a package and thought that I would nicely and neatly sort of transition from one thing to the next. Quite frankly, I did not know what I wanted to do, but knew that I wanted to go out on my own."

Isabelle decided to leave Pioneer and in January 1997 went to Evergreen Keystone Investment as chief investment officer. Unfortunately, that did not work out, and he shifted to Prospect Street Asset Management to run a closed-end fund that the firm had wanted to convert to an open-end fund.

That didn't work out, either, Isabelle decided after about a month.

"Some people, just to save face, will stay where they are. I think that that is stupid, so I said, 'That's it,' and I started my own company with two partners," he said.

And the rest, as they say, is history. Isabelle and two partners started their own firm, Ironwood Capital Management. In 1998 they launched the ICM/Isabelle Small Cap Value fund, which when we met in the summer of 2001 managed $140 million.

"Again I was baptized by the market. We launched the fund in May and had a couple of good months of performance. Then the Asian crisis hit, and the market got crushed," he said. "If you took a linear regression model and looked at cap sizes, here is how bad you did during that period: The smaller the cap size, the worse you did, and we got clobbered."

Isabelle believes that what helped him through the market was that the fund owned "very good" merchandise. The problem was that nobody wanted it.

"In the beginning, we had it tough. At one point we were down almost 30 percent and it was hard, but I knew that sticking with the right stocks would carry the fund through," he said.

Besides the mutual fund, Ironwood also manages about $120 million in separate accounts that are small-cap oriented and some more diversified portfolios as well. The company is built on the concept that it is preferable to have less internal staff and to let other people do the things they do best.

That's why Isabelle and a team of analysts do all the money management functions internally, his partners oversee administration and marketing, and outsourcing firms provide the rest of the services it needs to function.

"We have a tiny group at the top, our corporate overhead if you will, and all the rest of the functions are outsourced and everything is done in the virtual world," he said. "It works quite well and makes us more efficient, both from an operation standpoint and from a business one."

Today Isabelle continues to stick to his guns and manages money the same way as he did in California when he invested in the defense industry.

"I believe that you build a diversified portfolio through stock selection, and I don't have any preconceived notions about how to do it. I just try to keep an open mind and believe that if you have a good ability to decipher information and find anomalous situations, that is when you score," he said.

Isabelle, like most value investors, is always looking to buy something for nothing, especially when the market gives it away. He believes the only time the market gives it away, though, is when there is an anomaly and people believe one thing but something else actually is going on.

"When a company is forgotten and is doing okay but nobody cares, it is a possibility for us," he said. "You have to look at each company individually as if you are a competitor. You have to understand what the best economics are so that you know everything about the business and can determine at what point it makes sense for the company to be acquired, and then you can come up with a value for the security."

Isabelle's overall strategy is to go where the value is, regardless of the market sector or even if it appears to be a growth play.

"People have accused me of being a closet growth guy because I buy biotechs and other areas that are perceived to be growth stocks," he said. "My response is I am buying something for nothing, regardless of what it looks like and as long as it has real economics."

An example of his something-for-nothing strategy is the biotech company Sios, in which the fund made about seven times on its original investment.

Isabelle bought stock in the company for between $4 and $5 a share and it had $4 in cash on its books, meaning that he paid less than a dollar for the company's base business. He also got with it a third-party marketing force that was generating $40 million in sales and $10 million in operating income a year that nobody seemed to put a value on.

When Isabelle initially became interested in the stock there were two apparant drawbacks: that it had a management team with a fairly checkered past, and that the company had brought a drug to phase-three trials but the federal Food and Drug Administration had said, "Sorry, we can't approve this drug."

Isabelle and his team looked into the situation and found two very interesting things. First, it turned out that the FDA did not say the drug was not approvable, but rather that the protocols would not allow it to approve the drug; second, the company had brought on an entirely new management team.

"We checked out the management team and found that they were solid, and then when we understood the situation with the FDA we realized that the stock made sense," he said. "But if that was not enough, we also found that they were working on a congestive heart failure drug that they only needed to make minor changes to and most likely the drug would be approved. It basically became a no-brainer for us."

When Isabelle and I met in the summer of 2001, the stock was trading around $27 a share.

In areas where the business models are unproved, Isabelle

looks for companies with strong cash positions, ideas that offer great potential, and strong management. If it is a technology company, he wants it to be close enough to Boston so he can keep an eye on it.

"We like to be hands-on, so that we can fill in the blanks, if you will, by talking to other people who may be involved or have knowledge about what is going on and how it will be received in the marketplace," he said. "Everything we do is driven by fundamentals."

One of the ways Isabelle gets into trouble is when he finds a company that he believes has all the right ingredients but for some reason does not have, as he says, enough "grease to get to the goal line."

An example of a place where he was burned was a spin-off from a large paper company. Originally the spin-off had a market value of about $500 million. By the time Isabelle started looking at it, the value had dropped to $100 million, although it had $1 billion in sales.

"It turned out that even though things looked good, the management team was just not able to make things work, and eventually the company filed for bankruptcy," he said. "We got out before it filed—not that much before—and we took a beating. I still think that someday someone will make a killing on that company, because it has all the right elements. It just needs somebody husbanding the infrastructure, and nobody has yet."

Isabelle gets his investment ideas from various sources, including friends, former colleagues, and brokers who come to him. He likes to use his network of former colleagues around Boston, as well as around the country, as sounding boards once he finds something he thinks may be a good idea.

He recalls, "People used to make fun of me for reading *BusinessWeek*. They would say, 'What are you reading that for? There are no good ideas in there,' and my response always was and is, 'If *BusinessWeek* can show me the tip of the iceberg and it is white, then I will find out what is below the surface.' There are a lot of people and companies out there who make their living providing the Street with ideas, and we dialogue with them."

The current plan is to close the fund to new investors when it hits $500 million. Then Isabelle plans to open additional funds using other strategies. He would like to launch an all-cap special situations fund seeking to capture value from a lot of different angles, as well as a mid-cap fund and maybe even a micro-cap fund. He says he might even look at doing some regional offerings, like a New England fund—something that he could be "very hands-on" with, he says.

"I think that my experience with the large stocks will really help me over time with managing this portfolio and not only will allow us to grow this fund but will also provide us with an opportunity to add additional funds and products," he said. "The thing we have to be careful about is how we communicate our products to the public, and we have to make sure that we have the right talent to run the funds."

Isabelle believes that the mutual fund business is a relatively simple business in two parts: product and distribution. He feels that he represents the product side and has neither the interest nor the capital to build the sales side. As long as he continues to perform and stick to his convictions, he won't need to worry about that end.

"Unlike 15 years ago, there are very few undiscovered things out there. The way you make that work for you is by stretching your horizon," he said. "Today everybody wants everything to be right in front of his or her eyes. They are very myopic, so I believe that if you can see a little further than they can, that is where you get your acuity and that is how we will win. By win, I mean continue to perform stronger than the benchmarks and our competitors."

What I Think . . .

It appears from my meetings with Isabelle that he is really onto something. He has a unique approach to finding small-cap opportunities that will benefit investors for years to come.

One thing that is certain is that as his business grows and his assets under management increase, he will hire more people. The new staff will also be able to help him identify new markets. He doesn't strike me as a man who is going to have a problem giving up a little to get a lot. It was quite clear from our conversations that he really wants to see his company grow significantly over the next few years.

His experience working at Pioneer is really an asset to both present and future investors because he obviously knows how to build a business and understands that one person cannot do everything. Even for him, though, it probably won't be easy. That's why it's important for investors to pay attention to the firm's infrastructure and how it's evolving.

Over time, I believe Isabelle will branch out into many areas of the value market, and investors should follow his moves. He knows how to pick winners and he knows how to be successful. One thing that Isabelle offers that most other managers don't is that it's his company, it's his money, and it's his reputation that's on the line. I think that is a very important part of what drives Isabelle and the folks at Ironwood and also what makes them successful.

Marion Schultheis

For more than 20 years, Marion Schultheis has been analyzing stocks and managing money on Wall Street.

Schultheis did her undergraduate work in math at Rutgers University. Her first job after earning her MBA from the University of Minnesota was as an analyst covering electric utilities for American Express Advisors.

When we met in October 2001, she was managing more than $2.5 billion in a large-cap mutual fund and a mid-cap mutual fund for New York–based J. & W. Seligman & Co. She has been with Seligman since the mid-1990s.

As a managing director and portfolio manager, she heads Seligman's global growth team of seven investment professionals who focus on both domestic and international stocks. Three analysts cover specific industry sectors: health care, technology, and consumer goods. The other four focus on international equities on a more general basis.

"We believe that there are two main models for research," she said. "One is a pooled research department, which is what most firms have, where the analysts help all sorts of portfolio managers, ranging from growth to value and small-, mid-, and large-cap stocks. Then there is the way that we analyze investment opportunities, using a dedicated analyst for a specific product.

"Many fund managers don't want to give too much credit

to where they get their ideas, but I believe it is important to realize that the analysts on my team contribute significantly to the success of the portfolios," she continued. "I truly believe that people are either good at value or good at growth. One is very top-down oriented, and the other is bottom-up oriented and that's why it is hard to be good at both."

Schultheis thinks that two of the keys to her success are understanding her goal and her ability consistently to meet or exceed it.

"My goal is to beat my benchmark, as well as to be in the first quartile of my competitive group in terms of performance every year," she said. "If I do that, then over a three-year period everybody will be very happy with the portfolio."

This being the case, she believes that often her performance may not look so good in absolute terms but in relative terms she feels she is doing quite well. For example, in October 2001 one of her funds was down about 20 percent for the year. That is a poor result in absolute terms, but compared to the S&P 500, which was down 30 percent for the year, her performance was quite good.

"It seems that often CNBC and everybody else is not interested in talking about goals and if portfolio managers are achieving them, or what the level of risk of a specific portfolio is. Instead they focus simply on today," she said. "I believe that you have to look at the asset class, and as long as you are beating your benchmark and your peer group, you will be significantly beating the S&P."

Schultheis combines both top-down and bottom-up analysis of mid-cap and large-cap stocks.

"Our strategy consists of a sort of side-by-side approach to research, as opposed to a linear approach," she said. "If I were to make our process linear, then I would say that the first thing we would do is to pick the industry. I think that thinking and acting that way is a little too mechanized as opposed to what I do in reality."

Schultheis tries to figure out not only whether she wants to own a stock, but when to buy it, how long to hold it, and how much of it she wants in the portfolio. In most cases, she will allocate between 1 and 5 percent of a fund's assets to the company. The large-cap portfolio generally holds 50 stocks; the mid-cap portfolio, 60.

"I very rarely like to own less than 1 percent of a company because then I end up having too many names in the funds," she said. "I want to own a fairly concentrated group of companies."

Take, for example, Wal-Mart. Schultheis believes that for an individual investor owning the stock forever may make some sense, but as a portfolio manager, owning 3 or 4 percent of the company forever is not going to help meet her goals.

"It is not about owning a stock or not owning a stock; it is about how much you own at any given period," she said. "In large-cap, for example, everybody knows what the great names are. We know that Pfizer is a great name, that Wal-Mart is a great name; but the question is, when do you own these companies and how much of them do you own?"

She does not start the research process by looking to see whether the stock is cheap, but rather by studying the environment for the particular sector. So in looking at Wal-Mart, she would first see how retail stocks are doing relative to the equities market as a whole to project how the stock would do 12 to 18 months down the road.

"We look at the macro factors, things like GDP (gross domestic product), interest rates, and inflation. They're all part of the research process," she said. "I want to know if this is the time in the economic cycle to own a retail stock, and the only way to do that is to understand the current economic cycle."

After doing that, she looks at the fundamentals of the group, particularly supply and demand. In sectors like energy, she believes supply and demand issues are obvious, but it's a little harder to analyze them when it comes to retailers.

"When we are looking at retailers and want to evaluate supply-and-demand issues, we look at square footage," she said. "By looking at where square footage is being added and which companies are taking up the space, we can tell what type of environment the retail sector is experiencing and believes it will experience in the future."

There was a time when Schultheis and her team saw malls with two or three Sunglass Hut stores—a very bad sign. But as the malls changed, adding some stores and closing others, the team was able to forecast trends in the industry as well as to make predictions about individual stocks.

For example, over the past few years, Office Depot and Office Max both closed a lot of stores, so square footage in the office supply sector is down. When demand picks up, however, Schultheis believes the companies in that space are really going to rock.

"Today we are getting an amazing opportunity in the cruise line industry," she said. "Even before the events of September 11th, the industry had been suffering, and now it is in even worse shape. The supply-and-demand aspect of our research has helped us find opportunities, so that when the industry comes back we will be positioned to take advantage of it."

She uses her supply-and-demand findings to pinpoint companies that she believes will grow, regardless of market conditions.

"We want to watch for when there is too much supply," she said. "If there is, prices will come down and everyone will get hurt."

Coming into 2000, Schultheis avoided companies like Motorola, Nokia, and Ericsson. It was clear to her that there was too much supply and not enough demand for cellular phones, which meant that the companies were destined for trouble. Going into 2002, though, she believes that two years of disappointing sales of phones indicates pent-up demand and a significant number of new products, which makes the supply-and-demand balance attractive.

Schultheis also looks at the regulatory aspect of any industry. For example, at the time we met the lack of a head of the Food and Drug Administration was holding back the biotech and pharmaceutical sectors, she believed, by delaying the approval of new drugs.

"Regulatory issues have a significant impact in some sectors of the market," she said. "However, now that many areas have been deregulated, it is becoming less and less important."

Schultheis also looks at a company's relative earnings. Some industries grow faster than benchmarks, some grow slower, and some grow at varying levels, depending on the economic or market environment. She tries to find companies that will be the most attractive in the future, regardless of the environment.

"We start by looking at every single sector and then look at how they are weighted in our benchmark. Then, based on a 12-to-18-month time frame, we make a decision as to how we will weight them in our portfolio," she said. "We then try to determine which sectors are going to do the best and then determine within sectors which industries are going to do better, because we realize sectors are not homogenous."

By coming up with expectations for earnings over 12 to 18 months, Schultheis decides how to overweight or underweight a specific industry in the funds. Still, she will invest in some areas of the market, no matter how horribly they seem to be doing—for example, technology.

"Three areas of the market that we primarily invest in are technology, health care, and consumer cyclicals, which consist of about 75 percent of the assets under management at any one time," she said. "If all three went against me, I could do well on a relative basis, but our absolute returns would be horrible."

She continued, "I have to know what drives every industry. Understanding what is driving an industry allows us to make much more thorough decisions."

In 2000, for example, Schultheis moved much of the large-cap portfolio's assets out of energy. Although earnings there looked good and many of the stocks looked cheap, she believed that the price of oil was becoming more important than earnings.

"A lot of people held on to the energy stocks because they thought they were getting a bargain. We saw that things were not as good as they seemed and we got out," she said. "We knew that the price of the commodity is supply-and-demand driven and had little or nothing to do with the relative earnings of the industry or the company's growth. So we made a decision to get out."

Still, she considers earnings growth important. Even when things don't look good, because she is looking a year ahead she believes she can find opportunities that others miss.

"Take, for example, Carnival Cruise Lines. Right now the stock is at $22. I don't know if it is going to go to $17," she says, "but I am pretty sure that once all the dust settles and things get back to normal, a year or 18 months from now it will probably be between $35 and $40 a share. I know the management, I know the balance sheet, and I know that people will once again start taking cruises. Because I have a feel for the valuation and a good sense of the expectations, I can make a good decision."

By looking so far into the future, though, Schultheis often finds herself early to a position. In some cases that can cause problems.

"It will be six months or so before the numbers come out and people start paying attention to a company like Carnival," she said. "The question is not whether I am willing to be early, because the answer is yes; the question is, am I willing to own a lot and take on the risk in light of the current situation around the globe? I know that the situation cannot last forever and eventually people will start to travel again, but because people are still scared, I am going to limit my position."

When she finds a sector that looks attractive, she tries to find opportunities for both the large- and mid-cap portfolios. So, while Carnival Cruise Lines is a tourism stock for the mid-cap fund, for the large-cap fund she would look at a company like Hilton Hotels Corporation.

"If we decide we like a specific area of a sector and that it looks attractive, we will always try to find the company with the strongest balance sheet and avoid the smaller players," she said. "With cruise lines there are basically two dominant players, Royal Caribbean and Carnival. Because Carnival has the stronger balance sheet, we will go with it because in our opinion it is the best."

Schultheis works with her team to narrow sectors into areas that they believe are going to have the most growth.

"Today we are looking at three specific areas of the health

care industry: biotechnology, medical devices, and pharmaceutical companies. We believe over a three-to-five-year time frame they are going to work better than other areas of the industry," she said.

In the large-cap portfolio, Schultheis tries to limit the amount of turnover to less than 100 percent. In most cases, she expects to hold a stock for 12 months, but because some tend to move quickly, she often takes some profits and reduces her positions.

"Last year the independent power companies grew 100 percent in the first eight months of the year, hitting our three-year target price for many of the positions," she said. "So we had to get out of some of the positions, take the profits, and reallocate the assets."

Schultheis sets a stock's target price based on her calculations of the company's expected earnings two years out from the time she starts looking at it. When a stock hits her target, she sells it.

"If you have a company growing at 30 percent a year and it looks expensive in 2002, you don't need it to expand; you will get it naturally," she said. "On average we want to get one and a half percent on our positions over the broad market. So if the S&P is expected to grow at 8 percent or 10 percent, we would expect our positions to grow at least 12 percent or 15 percent during the same time period."

By screening industries instead of individual stocks, she is able to spot trends that allow her to forecast earnings growth for three years. Once she finds an industry within a sector that looks attractive, she then looks at the fastest-growing companies within the industry group as potential investment opportunities.

"We believe that biotech and some niches in technology are going to give you 20 percent to 30 percent growth," she said.

"Then we look at what we are paying for that and figure it out from there.

"We don't want to pay high prices, but in this environment we are getting some really attractive niches in some fast-growing areas," she continued. "And because we had bubbles in certain areas, people are afraid to get back in. That leaves us a lot of opportunities."

Schultheis said that when it comes to biotech, she often has a problem keeping a stock for longer than a year or even six months because competitors are moving so rapidly in and out of the names causing the stocks to swing widely in price.

"The swings in biotech are huge. For the month of October a number of our biotech stocks are up 20 percent," she said. "So what should I do? I can't just sit there. If I am 15 percent in biotech and my benchmark is at 10 percent, I have to trim the positions to get in line with the benchmark. I do not want to be underweight for the group because I still believe in the group for the next 18 months."

Along with fundamental and quantitative analysis of the companies, she also spends a lot of time focusing on understanding management and analyzing its strengths and weaknesses.

"In 100 percent of the cases, we rank the managements of every company we are interested in on a scale of 1 to 10," she said. "Our process focuses on the strengths of management teams, so that when we own a stock and we get bad news we are able to make an educated decision based on the strength of management, instead of a reactionary one."

She ranks management by sectors, so in the health care industry Pfizer and Eli Lilly are 10s, as are the people at Wal-Mart and General Electric in the retail sector. Everyone else is ranked relative to their sector's best manager. She does not look at any company with management ranked lower than 8.

"We try to understand how management is looking at the business by asking them questions that are more long-term-oriented than short-term," she said. "Recently we were at a meeting with a medical device company's officials. They were explaining that they finally had rounded out their line of stents, and now doctors would be willing to buy the entire line, while six months earlier doctors were not interested because the line was not complete. At the meeting, some of my competitors were asking all about the product and trying to understand how this stent was different and how it worked. My question was, 'Why did it take you so long to round out your product line?' The answer to a question like that will tell me if they are going to run into a similar problem down the road."

Schultheis ranks company management according to sector because she believes that it is unfair to compare the management of Wal-Mart to the management of General Electric. The key for her is to understand management's focus, vision, and execution of strategy in order to understand how the company is going to expand its market share.

"We want to understand how we can measure a company's strategy, and then what we do is actually go back and measure them to see if they are truly executing on their strategy," she said. "We don't judge them on what Wall Street thinks; we judge them on what *we* think. Often we end up liking the managements, and in turn the stocks, of companies that Wall Street doesn't like."

One thing that she tries to avoid is getting caught up in the information flow that surrounds many companies, causing the price of their stock to move up and down without warning.

"Paying attention to the information can really make things difficult," she said. "Last week, for example, there was some really negative information about a large drug company and the stock dropped 4 percent in one day, which for this company was a big move. If we had paid attention to the news we would have avoided it, but because we understood that the news was relatively meaningless in the big picture, it turned into a buying opportunity for us.

"Unlike most of the Street, which thought the opportunity had changed for the negative, we understood that it was actually a positive and were able to take advantage of it," she continued. "I think from an investor's perspective it is important to understand where the ideas are coming from and how they are being executed."

One thing that helps Schultheis make investment decisions is understanding where the spark for growth will come from.

"We all know Wal-Mart, for example, is a good stock and that the consumer likes going to the stores, but we want to know what is left," she said. "We want to know what is going to drive the company; we want to know what is not yet in the price of the stock and what the catalyst is going to be to make the stock move.

"If I can't find the catalyst that will allow me to outperform with the stock, I am pretty sure that I don't want to be in the name," she continued. "I am wasting the opportunity when I can see the catalysts in other stocks and take advantage of them."

★ ★ ★

What I Think . . .

It seems that Schultheis cares more about her performance numbers than most of the other people profiled. It is safe to say that all of them are interested in performing well relative to their peers, but Schultheis is the most focused on the numbers. This is where she adds an enormous amount of value for her investors.

I believe most will do well in the long run by putting money in her hands. The only problem, as with some of the other managers, is that at some point the funds will reach capacity. I've found that large fund complexes focus on increasing their assets so much that eventually performance suffers and in the end the investor gets hurt.

Some investors may also cringe at the fact that these are load funds. I don't think it really matters. What matters is management, and if management is good and does what it is supposed to do the loads are well worth the costs. Isn't it better to pay for service that you get than to do it yourself and pay with the lack of performance?

Gerald Frey

Gerry Frey got into the money management business late in life—"after growing up"—at the ripe old age of 34.

Earlier he had worked for an engineering firm that asked him to move from New York City to Minnesota—in the middle of winter, no less. Luckily he met a money manager named Bob Kern who offered him a research job at Chase Investors, enabling him to stay in the city.

"Bob sort of said to me that he thought I was smart, that I knew how companies worked, and he thought that I would be good at researching stocks," Frey said.

At Chase, he worked with Bob and his team managing the small-cap growth funds. Over the next few years he progressed rapidly up the money management food chain until finally in 1986 he left to set up a money management business at Morgan Grenfell. Again he focused on small-cap stocks and, in particular, on technology stocks, with a research emphasis on capital spending.

"It was a very interesting time," he said. "When new stocks came public, for the most part they were in areas that were not traditional, and we often would sit around the table and look at the new issues and say, 'Okay, here is the biotech stock. Does anyone know anything about biology?' Because I majored in biology for one year, I got to cover it."

In 1996, Frey and his family moved to Philadelphia when his wife got a job at a hospital there.

"I knew someone in the city who had been managing a small growth product, who was trying to grow the business and needed some help managing the fund," he said. "It was one of the those things where he said to me that he needed someone to manage the fund so he could go out and market it. It really fit with what I wanted to do."

Frey became co-manager and worked to shape the fund from a retail product to one that could attract institutional money. He added staff, management tools, and infrastructure. Nine months later, his partner and some others left to form another money management firm, and he was left in charge.

Today he is the senior vice president/senior portfolio manager of the Equity Growth Group of Delaware Investments, overseeing $5 billion for both retail and institutional investors. The firm offers small-, mid-, and large-cap funds, as well as some sector funds, all of which are focused on growth stocks.

Frey is in charge of the entire growth stock operation. He works with a very close-knit group of seven, each of whom is directly related to the investment process, plus a four-member support staff. Delaware Investments is the investment arm of Lincoln Financial Group, the insurance company. It offers a range of funds in various investment styles, including bonds, value stocks, and real estate investment trusts. For the most part, the funds invest 99 percent of their assets, long only, in U.S.-based stocks. They do not use options and in general are 100 percent invested at all times. The funds are sold primarily through brokerages and financial intermediaries, as well as through Lincoln Financial's network.

Frey believes that people need to be held accountable for their actions. All seven portfolio persons are responsible for their own investments. Not only are they responsible, but also they had better have conviction about each investment.

"A lot of my job is to make sure that people execute what they say they are going to do. If they can't or are having problems, then I may intercede and tell them, 'You know what? This is really not working, and we'd better sell it,' and if they can't do it, I will," he said. "They need to be able to move on, so by my getting involved I can help them move forward and not dwell on mistakes."

Frey said that one of the characteristics that have led to the firm's success has been that he has tried to create a team atmosphere.

"We are all very collegial. It is not just one person making the investment decisions who is saying, 'Okay this is the way the world is,'" he said. "The reality is I have the authority to do that, but if you do that consistently, you probably are not going to have anyone who wants to work with you. People are not going to stay if they are not given responsibility. The skill is to develop a level of give-and-take that works for everybody.

"Our job is to be successful so that we can grow the business," he continued. "The only way that is going to happen is if we have good people, and good people stay around only if they are respected."

Frey's team approach begins with the hiring process. He doesn't use headhunters, but relies on people he knows in the business or friends of people he knows in the business to recruit his staff.

"Most of the people on the team are midcareer professionals who are not just right out of school but rather have worked at very good money management firms," he said. "We try to recruit people who are far enough along in their careers that they know what they are doing. To complement them, we hire people who are at the very early stages of their careers who really don't have a huge responsibility in the investment process but work alongside the rest of the team to learn the business. As time moves on they get more and more responsibility."

He tries to teach the younger members that they need to understand the investments that they make and how to buy them at the right time. The volatility in the wake of the attacks on the Pentagon and the World Trade Center also caused Frey to focus on teaching his people to be able to continue to execute on their ideas.

"We really tried to work with people to teach them not to freeze up and just sit there and watch the monitors, but rather to make decisions that are appropriate for investors," he said. "Look, right now everything is down. The question we have been asking is, 'Will you sell XYZ now, and possibly take the tax loss, and reinvest the proceeds in something that, going forward, may have better investment potential and in turn upgrade the quality of the portfolio?' "

He continued, "This is how we have been coping with the markets during these volatile times. It is not much fun to do this right now; but, look, there are always issues. Sure, things are bad, but if we can teach people how to operate in this type of environment, well, in two or three years from now when something else happens, whether it's the economy or something else, they will be prepared. Something always happens to affect the way markets act. The question is: Are you prepared to react and do you know what to do?"

Although Frey has veto power over his group's investment ideas, he tries not to exert his power because he feels it will weaken the team. He also focuses his efforts on the stock selection process, meeting with the managements of companies and designing portfolios, rather than spending time on the marketing side of the business.

"I think our system works because I manage money also and because I oversee the whole portfolio. You have to lead by example. You have to make investment decisions that make sense. I am right there along with everybody else," he said. "I have been called by the financial networks [to be a market commentator] many times, and I always refuse because I find it really hard to believe that someone can get on CNBC and say anything really intelligent in 30 seconds and have the viewers walk away with an idea that is going to help them."

Obviously, even with Frey's experience, he had never encountered markets like the ones in the wake of the attacks. Because of his experience, though, he believes that he and his team were better prepared to deal with the markets when they reopened.

"I don't think anyone has ever seen markets like this before. I mean, there are different levels of it—like 1987, 1991 with the Iraqi war, and the collapse of Long Term Capital Management in 1998. People have seen those things, but each one of these tragic events or financial occurrences has its own different parameters around it," he said. "To be short-term investors right now really does not make any sense, and the problem is that most people are not long-term investors. The only way to make it through any time of crisis is to be a long-term investor."

Frey meets with his team at least once a week, and often much more frequently.

"CNBC would like us all to believe that the investment process is a minute-by-minute, tick-by-tick business, but the reality is that it is much more extended. The world does not change that dramatically in a day," he said. "Obviously on September 11 it did, but in general it really does not. What we try to do is to find good companies, find good businesses, and make investments in those businesses by trying to get the best prices possible and build broadly diversified portfolios.

"I can't tell people that I am the world's expert on every business that is out there. Sure, I can say that I understand retailers, for example, but am I the best retail person? Probably not," he continued. "It's same thing for technology, so in order to get this expertise, we have people who focus on different areas. That is all they do, and they come up with ideas that are worthy of the portfolio."

Frey said that by operating this way, he not only is getting the best from his staff but also doing right by his investors.

"I would like to tell people that I am the greatest superstar manager in the world, and I may believe that I am, but probably I am not. By getting a group of people who work well together, if I get hit by a truck tomorrow your assets are safe," he said.

There are generally not that many individual ideas that

make it to the portfolio, but rather a consensus of a few members of the team before a purchase is made. In some cases, an individual's ideas may represent 10 percent of the portfolio—five positions each worth 2 percent. The first thing the team does is try to decide which are the best companies and which have the most immediate upside potential.

"We often do switch programs within the various areas of responsibility to make sure we are in the right stock at the right time," he said. "We also look at how we are weighted and why we are weighted versus the various indexes. If we are grossly overweighted or underweighted, why? I don't have a problem being over or under—I just want to know why. A lot of people who manage money have a predilection to certain industries or sectors, and when you look at their portfolios, they are really sector funds."

Frey does not want to be one of them; he wants to stick with what he tells people he does: manage broad-based growth-oriented funds.

"We don't have a sci-fi fund or a fund that is 100 percent technology," he said. "So what we do is we sit down as a group and try to understand what is going on in various areas and make decisions based on what we think is the right thing to do at that moment."

At the time we met, for example, the technology experts were saying that although the stocks were dramatically off their highs, bringing their price-earnings (P/E) ratios down to more reasonable levels, some of the businesses still did not make sense, because the fundamentals of the companies were not attractive.

"We are looking to put money in the technology [companies], because the valuations are good, but what we have to do is wait and see if the fundamentals are coming around," he said.

"There are many cheap stocks out there that represent a huge universe of names. They did not get into that universe on purpose; the majority of them sank there, and probably many of them will never return to anything meaningful. Our job is to find the successful companies that can come up from that pile."

To invest in the successful companies and hold them for a period of time is where Frey believes his team creates value for investors.

"If I buy a company with a market cap of, say, $500 million or $1 billion that is on its way to, say, $5 billion, I am creating value for my investors," he said. "So we want to find these types of ideas and hold them for a significant amount of time."

Frey said that the key is to find good companies and never try to trade down on quality.

"We try to avoid selling something just because there may be something cheaper out there," he said. "You need to stay with the best companies, because over time they will be the ones that perform for the portfolio."

One stock that fits that bill is Kohl's Corporation. The Wisconsin-based retailer has been part of Delaware's portfolio since Frey joined the firm in 1996.

"They have continued to execute and execute incredibly well. Sure, the economic environment affects them as much as it does everybody else, but they continue to gain market share, and they have built a successful business," he said. "Things like that over periods of time are what drives performance. That is just one example of the companies we have in the portfolio."

Another stock that continues to add a significant amount of performance to the portfolio is Doral Financial, which dominates the mortgage business in Puerto Rico.

"The company is very successful, it is very well run, and it has been a good stock over a period of time," he said. "The key is to understand if it is a good company and if they are going to be able to grow their business over time."

Frey and his team spend a lot of time meeting with the managements of companies they own and ones that they are interested in.

"There is a lot of legwork that goes into making a decision. Our people involved have the expertise, they have done it for a long time, they know what is going on, and they know what questions to ask," he said. "Things they ask are as basic as 'How does the business work?' and 'What are the margins?' and as sophisticated as 'What are the cash flows?' and 'How do you expect to grow the business?' "

He explained, "We try to cover all the things that we think are necessary to understand the business. Sure, we are interested in the company's P/E ratio and its earnings expectations, but we are also interested in how management plans on taking the company forward in the next three, four, or five years."

Frey said he does not believe that people can trade their way to success through small-cap investing.

He generally runs a very focused portfolio with about 75 positions. The portfolio is dependent on stock selection; he doesn't simply throw something on the wall and hope that it sticks.

He thinks that often investors get so wrapped up in making funds fit in a style box or some sort of ranking system that they lose sight of what the fund manager is trying to do.

"Suppose I own a stock that has a $500 million market cap and it goes to $1 billion and someone from Morningstar calls me and says, 'Hey, it looks like you are no longer a small-cap manager. You are more of a mid-cap manager.' So then I sell the position to get back in the small-cap box, but the stock goes from $1 billion to $2 billion or $3 billion. Well, I really have not done any favors for my investors," he said. "So instead of focusing on how people view us, we just try to do what we said we would from the beginning, which is to continually produce solid returns year after year."

Frey looks at his job as what it is and not much more.

"I am a pretty quiet person and really don't enjoy getting up in front of a large group of people to discuss our strategy. Obviously there are some times when it is necessary, but for the most part I leave it to the marketing and sales teams to communicate our message," he said. "I am a simple guy from a small town. This is just my job. Some people build buildings, and I happen to build portfolios and try to make money for people."

Frey said that his investment style was formed very much during the time he spent working with Bob Kern and categorizes himself as his protégé.

"Bob and I became very close friends, and he really provided me with the foundation that I have used to build and hone my money management skills to what they are today," he said. "Because of the time we spent together, I am able not only to be a better manager but also to understand the importance of teaching others the trade so that they, too, can manage more effectively."

★ ★ ★

What I Think . . .

Gerald Frey is the epitome of old-time (pre-1990s bull market, that is) money managers.

Back then, there were few managers other than, say, Peter

Lynch or John Bogle whom retail investors recognized. Now, as media coverage of the markets has exploded, so has the number of managers doubling as market commentators. It's rare to find a manager who doesn't seek publicity. Frey is one of the rare ones. He is focused solely on managing money, has little or no interest in marketing his product, and doesn't want to be another talking head on CNBC or CNNfn. He is basically content with what he's doing.

Frey is the type of manager I would want to manage my money because he seems so even-keeled. I think he is a rare bird in today's exhibitionistic flock of fund managers.

Paul Blaustein

Paul Blaustein is a money manager who thinks swinging for the fences might work in baseball, but it never works when it comes to picking stocks.

"It has gotten to the point that being in the middle of the pack in the performance ratings has no value," he said, "so you might as well swing for the fences and try to be number one. That is what the ranking systems drive people to try to be, and I think that focusing on things like that really does not work in the long run."

In 2000, Lipper ranked him number 1 for seven straight months in his category. To him it made no sense.

"They were focusing on a rolling 12 months, and they were not looking at the longer-term record, which is what they should have been doing," he said. "What does it tell you when you look at an artificial 12-month period ending on the last day of the prior month? It really does not tell you very much."

Blaustein says that there is no way to overcome the ranking systems, so instead of worrying about where he stands, he focuses on what he sees as his job: to make the portfolio perform.

"My experience both here and at other firms has taught me that the most important thing is to put up solid performance numbers. All I am trying to do, as consistently as possible, is to beat the S&P 500 for a meaningful time period," he said. "If you do that consistently over the long term, you will have an outstanding record. The objective is not to be among the top 10 percent or in the top decile in a given year; the objective is to try to sustain the fund's performance over the long term."

His aim, however, is never to fall far below the midpoint of the rankings and generally to be in the top quartile.

"The value of consistency in a world that is churning a great deal is that the longer the time horizon, the better you look competitively," he said.

Blaustein's first job on the Street was as a securities analyst at the Bank of New York, where he covered many sectors of the market. He joined the bank after getting an undergraduate degree from Brooklyn College and an MBA from Columbia University.

"I got into this business because it seemed like what I wanted to do. The more and more people I talked to about it agreed that it was the right thing for me to do, so I sort of did it," he said.

From the Bank of New York he went across Wall Street to Bankers Trust, where he also was an analyst covering multiple sectors. He then went to work at Oppenheimer Capital for 11 years, covering a number of sectors and advancing to portfolio manager.

In 1997 he joined Whitehall Asset Management, where he is a senior managing director, managing $300 million in the firm's growth fund, its growth and income fund, and a few separate accounts.

Blaustein thinks his success comes from understanding that knowing a little about a lot is much more important than knowing a lot about a little.

"After a while, the value of knowing more is very, very limited," he said. "Plus, if you are really going to invest, you don't want to know everything about the automobile industry. What you want to know is, how do you value the company, and in turn what are auto companies worth? What are the similarities of these companies versus other companies?"

He believes that the only way to value something is to look at what alternatives are selling for at a specific point in time and in that environment.

"If you were going to buy a house, you would look at other houses in the neighborhood to get an idea of what something is worth," he explained. "I think that is what you have to do as an investor. It is baloney when people tell you that they know what a company is worth. There is no such thing as what something is worth. Something is worth only what someone is willing to pay for something right now, and the only way to get a view of what something is worth is by doing comparative values of something at the same point in time.

"To pick a number out of the air and say that, no matter what the environment is, this is the underlying value of a company is absurd," he said. "It's like the old Henny Youngman joke; 'How's your wife?' 'Compared to what?' The only way you can really do a valuation at a given point in time is to compare it to alternatives that exist in the market."

One theme that seems to be a driving force behind his success is that of freedom to learn and to work and basically to do what he wants to do in managing the portfolio.

"I have a great interest in knowing a little bit about everything and knowing everything about absolutely nothing," he said. "So two, maybe three, great appeals of this job are that, first, you don't have to know everything about anything. In fact it is a disadvantage, because if you know so much about something or try to know so much about something, then you are incapable of taking action and making a decision. Second, virtually everything is relevant, so anything you are interested in you do not have to feel guilty about pursuing, because it probably is relevant in some way. And, third, you get to meet a lot of very interesting people. I mean, if you went to work in the finance department of a large financial institution, what is the likelihood that you would ever meet the CFO or CEO of the company? Probably never. If you go to work in the investment business, you probably meet a CFO or CEO the first day."

Blaustein said that, of all the people he has met in his career, the one who has influenced him the most was Jack Welch of General Electric Company.

"I can't think of any person alive that I have learned more from than Jack Welch," he said. "Having met him was a wonderful thing, and I can't think of very many jobs that would have provided me the opportunity to meet him or people who try to be similar to him."

Blaustein said that one of the most unfortunate things about being an investor in the stock market as compared to being the CEO of a company is that you have less control over a situation.

"No matter what you do and no matter how hard you try, you can't make a stock go up," he said. "You have to make the most of the advantages that are presented to you, with the thought that over time the economy grows, it does not shrink, so values over the long term or any reasonable amount of time will go up."

Blaustein works with a group of five people who look for ideas for the funds. The group is not quantitatively orientated, meaning that its members do not use statistical screening tools but rather rely on their experience.

"Most of what we buy represents things that we have been familiar with over the years," he said. "Of course, as you grow older you are trying to add some new companies to your stock of what we call back-burner ideas or inventory, but basically that is what we are doing. We are dealing with companies that we have known over significant periods of time, managements that we are well aware of, where we think we understand the company very, very well."

Retail investors, Blaustein believes, don't know as much as they need to to make good decisions. Of course, from the institutional side, he is able to learn more about a company than, say, someone who owns only 100 shares. He also has the advantage of knowing management and the company for a long time and so can see the future by interpreting the past.

"I like to understand the characteristics of the business, the type of performance that is possible in the business, the management, their perspective on the business, what their strategy is, and what tools and tactics they use to carry it out," he said. "Time becomes a leveraging factor. That is, if you watch something and are intimately involved with it over a long period of time, then you can understand it better."

Blaustein's objective is to invest in a limited number of companies and to understand them better than anyone else does. Typically, the funds keep between 35 and 40 stocks in their portfolios, with a turnover rate that averages about 30 percent a year.

"Essentially, we are not playing the stock market. We happen to be investing in companies that happen to have stocks that are traded," he said. "We are really interested in the companies that we invest in and are not in it for a quick hit. That makes it easier for us to understand the company and ask questions that management will actually think are good questions and actually answer."

There are times, however, when Blaustein's analysis does not come to the same conclusion as management's, and he passes up the opportunity.

"It comes down to either that they are wrong or we are wrong, and in either case it means we don't understand the business, and we do not want to be involved at that point," he said. "Management, for the most part, likes dealing with investors like us, but we are also sufficiently cynical that we are not going to necessarily accept the industry's view of itself. We are going to be very, very critical, but we try to be accurate. The objective is not to be needlessly conservative when there is a great business and we recognize that it is a great business."

While most people consider Whitehall to be too small to be significant, Blaustein believes that works to his advantage.

"Typically, very, very large money management firms try to use their scale and their power to get information from people that is not readily available. They are not really trying to understand the business, and often they have more rapid turnover of personnel than we do," he said. "I think managements appreciate the fact that we are not trying to get them to tell us something that they are not telling somebody else. We are trying to really understand what is there, when our competitors don't really care."

Blaustein thinks most of his competitors are focused on trying to forecast the quarter's earnings or doing some "very naive" analysis that says that this company historically sold at a 10 to 40 percent premium to the S&P 500 multiple and it is now selling at a 5 percent premium so it is clearly a buy. What they don't ask is when did it sell at 10 and 40 and was that fact ever meaningful and has the situation changed?

"I don't agree with the way most people manage money, but I will say something that I think is true of every endeavor: There are people who go about it the right way and there are people who go about it the wrong way," he said. "I strongly believe that most of the people in our business are relatively intelligent people, but trying to be smarter than everybody else doesn't really work for many people."

Blaustein's strategy is to look at the big picture and not worry as much about the most recent quarterly results. Sure, he would like his companies to make their numbers, but he also understands that sometimes things happen.

"I would like to think that when a company does not meet my expectations it is because of external causes, because external causes are beyond the control of management and are more likely to change," he said. "If the problem is in the company, then it is much less likely that things are going to change and it is much harder to change management."

Blaustein believes that most managements focus on shifting the blame for the shortfall rather than dealing with the problem that caused it.

"What underlies our approach is to really understand the business. I am a great believer that, despite everything I have said about Jack Welch, the business is generally more important than the management," he said. "A great manager with a bad business is still a bad business, and I don't really want to own a bad business with the best management in the world. I would love to have both [a great business and the best management], but I will settle for a Grade A business with a Grade B manager."

Generally he believes a Grade A business wasn't built by bad management, although bad management may have taken over later. Usually he is looking at companies with managements that have been so responsible for the building up of the business that he really thinks that they are Grade A managers as well.

"It gives us a real sense of reassurance," he said, "because the world does change and you really need good management to be astute enough to sense where the changes are and recognize them before the competition does and make the necessary changes in the business."

Blaustein said that he believes most of the sell-off that the market experienced in the wake of the terrorist attacks was the result of uncertainty in the market.

"People know that there is stuff out there, but they don't know what it is. Therefore they are afraid—not afraid of getting hurt physically but afraid of how long the recession is going to last or the uncertainty will remain," he said. "The hardest part is that people knew before the attack there was a lot that they did not know, and now they know there is even more that they don't know. I think that is what has been scaring people and pushing the market lower."

Blaustein said that what he did to shore up the portfolio during the downturn was very similar to what he would have done in any bear market: look for great assets that have taken a hit and estimate when the industries would return to normal.

"You have got to assess, in terms of price and nature of business, when the effect will wear off," he said. "The entire travel and entertainment industry will be down in the near term, because companies like Disney and Carnival are not going to come back as fast as a company like Viacom, which is basically dealing with a decrease in advertising. We need to position the portfolio for the turnaround."

Blaustein said it is easier to operate in a down market, because it is easier to find something to buy.

"One of the things that happens when you have sharp moves in the market is that everything does not move down together, and you sort of reshuffle the relative values. Since what we are doing is trying to benefit by inappropriate relative values, it gives us more opportunity," he said. "There are companies that will go down because this quarter is at risk but that's all. There is nothing wrong with the company, the business is intact, and they will be fine. They just won't earn as much money in this quarter or maybe next quarter as people thought they would, but in the end their model works."

Another thing that he believes hurt some companies during the volatility was not the attack on the World Trade Center but the fact the people finally realized that many companies did not have a business and that it didn't make sense to own a lot of the stocks.

"We are trying to buy great companies at reasonable prices," he said. "And that type of environment provided us with more of an opportunity to find them."

As an investor, Blaustein is always looking for prices to go lower to uncover opportunities.

"Yes, it is nice for my investors when prices go up, because they think that they are richer," he said. "But when prices go down we can buy them more assets at better prices."

He believes that he isn't smarter than other money managers

or that he has more talent, for that matter, but rather that he has a different approach that they haven't explored yet.

"I don't want to do what everyone else is doing because then I would have to be smarter than they are. So as long as I can do things that they have not thought of doing, then I don't have to be smarter than they are," he said.

What Blaustein and his team focus on for their portfolios is what makes a good business.

"As an investor, we are trying to participate in the progress or growth of the economy," he said. "Generally, the economy is going to grow most of the time, and the stock market is going to go up a lot more of the time than it is going to go down. On balance, it is going to go up because it reflects the growth in the economy. So what we are really trying to do is to find some good things—businesses that are growing, [companies that] have a high rate of return on capital, and companies that have sustainability—so that we can benefit over time."

Blaustein looks at the 5- or 10-year record to find companies that show what he calls "competitive dominance." Then he tries to figure out why.

"I want to know why the customer prefers their product to someone else's or why the customer would have difficulty or incur a cost to stop buying their product and buy somebody else's product," he said. "If I can understand those factors, then I can determine if it makes sense for the portfolio."

One thing that is important to Blaustein is scale. For example, according to him, Microsoft sells 19 copies of Windows for every copy of the Mac OS operating system that is sold by Apple. This suggests that over time Microsoft can invest more in improving Windows than Apple can in improving its system. Maybe, then, it makes sense to use Windows rather than

Mac OS, because in five years Windows will most likely improve more.

"The big differentiator is often information, which is a fixed cost," he said. "Whether you sell a hundred million copies of an operating system or five million, the cost of developing it is the same, making your per-unit costs very, very low [if you sell a hundred million]. So if I spend 10 percent per unit on research and development, as Apple does, I am still spending twice as much as the competition. Once you get into a dominant position, there are a lot of ways to sustain it."

It is hard, in Blaustein's opinion, to reach a dominant position in commodity-type businesses, so he tries to avoid them.

"In trying to understand what a business is worth, [we ask:] What kind of performance is it capable of producing? Has it produced that level of performance? If so, is it sustainable? If not, why not? These are the types of things we want to know about a company," he said. "The longer you look at a company over time, the more confident you can become in your decision to own it."

One company in particular that seems to fit this mold is Wal-Mart. Blaustein has owned the stock for quite some time and believes that year after year the company gets better and better. He thinks that Wal-Mart beats all of its competitors because customers do not want to be disappointed, and as a retailer Wal-Mart does not disappoint. The prices are better, the merchandise is in stock, the stores are cleaner, and the people are friendlier.

"Wal-Mart's success leads to the bankruptcies of its competitors simply because Wal-Mart does it better than anyone else," he said. "It is an example of how management cares, understands its job, executes on it, and in turn makes the company stronger by simply doing what they are paid to do."

Blaustein tries to experience companies as a customer and then relays his impressions to management to see what their reaction is. That's his way of gauging their commitment to the business.

"If a company does not value feedback from their customers or the relationships between customers and an employee, then they really have no idea what sort of business they are in," he said. "I remember speaking to the CEO of Home Depot, and he told me that the most important thing to remember about his business was that it was a relationship business. 'Everything that is sold in our stores they can buy elsewhere,' he said, 'and we need to establish a relationship that makes the customers come to us first when they want that merchandise. If they don't want to come to the store, if they do not prefer coming to our store, they are not going to come to our store, and we will lose the sale.' It comes to blocking and tackling, and customers vote with their feet!"

When it comes to evaluating companies, Blaustein tries to take the approach of a management consultant, saying if he can understand the business, what it can produce, and how it accomplishes it, he can determine whether it makes sense to buy the stock.

"It is like a black box. The historical record tells you what it produced; now we have to go figure out what is in the black box and how it did it and what it is likely to do in the future," he said. "I don't think that there are that many people looking at things like we do. Those who do tend to be classified as value investors and they are looking at bad companies. There are very few people who do it with good companies like we do."

What I Think . . .

Like Frey, Blaustein is one of a rare breed, simple but elegant. And while—unlike Frey—he is often quoted in the press or seen on television, he is more than a talking head. Blaustein capitalizes on his strengths and compensates for his weaknesses. He seems to have a unique interest in taking in as much as he can and appears to be constantly learning. Still, he is careful never to get bogged down and is able to focus on many subjects—industries—at once, making his portfolio quite dynamic.

In the late fall of 2001, I went to visit my little brother, Josh, in Los Angeles. I had forgotten to pack enough underwear, so Friday afternoon I went to Marshalls in Studio City to buy some. The store was in dreadful disarray. All I could think of was what Blaustein had said about how management's not caring trickles down to employees on every level and what that means for the company and its stock.

It was at that point that I really understood how Blaustein looks at companies and how he makes investment decisions.

Scott Black

When Scott Black looks at a potential investment, it has to be a good business with a high return on equity, and, most important, he must be able to buy it cheaply.

"Basically, I am following the original principles of Ben Graham," he said from his office that looks out over Boston

Harbor and Logan International Airport. "We are buying a business. We have no interest in the piece of paper that represents the company."

Black, who got his undergraduate degree at Johns Hopkins University and an MBA at Harvard Business School, launched his money management firm, Delphi Management Inc., in 1979 with one client: Sunkist Growers, the Florida fruit and produce cooperative.

"I was working in California for Bill O'Neil, the stock market guru and founder of the newspaper *Investor's Business Daily*, and a consultant asked me to visit with the people of Sunkist to give them a prospective portfolio. The original four stocks were the Interpublic Group, GEICO Corporation, Ogilvy & Mather, and the Washington Post Company. They agreed with me that they were good ideas, and eventually they became a client," he said. "Things were a lot different back then. The market was much more inefficient, and these companies were really great franchises selling at good prices."

Since then, Delphi has grown significantly. In the fall of 2001 when we met, Black had just under $1.5 billion under management in separate accounts and was managing the Delphi Value Fund, a no-load mutual fund for retail investors. Sunkist is still a client.

"When I first started the company, I told the consultants that once I had 20 institutional clients I would quit and no longer take on new investors,"[3] he said. "By the end 1994 we had a full complement of 20 institutional clients, and, while other people were focused on growing their businesses, we were intellectually honest and we stopped taking new clients."

Black devotes 99 percent of his time to securities research and portfolio management. He does not spend a lot of time doing presentations or handling accounts. He realizes the importance of those areas, but he believes that good performance is more important.

"One of the reasons we keep a low profile is because we know that if we get too big, we will not be able to execute our strategy," he said. "When you get so big, you have to move up in market capitalization, which is the most efficient side of the stock market and does not present as many opportunities."

Most people come to Delphi through word of mouth. In the past few years the firm has taken on some very large investors—high-net-worth individuals and families. For them, the minimum investment is $10 million. Retail investors can get in for $1,000 through the mutual fund.

"Regardless of the size of the account we use the same strategy across the board, because that is really what sets us apart from other managers, and it is what people are paying for," he said.

Black breaks every investment decision into two steps. The first is to determine whether the potential investment is a good business; the second, to determine whether he can buy it at a good price.

To start the process, Black looks at a series of what he calls quantitative factors.

"The most important thing to us is return on equity," he said. "We like a company to earn at least 15 percent on book [value]. In truth, however, our average company earns between 17 and 18 percent on book; and if it is a cyclical company, it is going to have to earn at least 15 percent on book during good times." Book value is the value of the assets, calculated as actual cost less any allowances for depreciation. Book value may be more or less than market value.

Once he finds a company that meets his return-on-equity requirements, he looks for the ability to grow both revenue and profits over three to five years at a significantly faster rate than inflation.

"The bulk of our companies grow at 11, 12, or 13 percent," he said. "It is unlikely that we will have a 40 percent grower, because we are a low P/E, price-to-book kind of buyer, and that is where the difference is. Our companies really grow businesses.

"People make a mistake," he continued. "They think that value is separate from growth. The key is to buy companies that have good growth dynamics—but you buy them at value."

In the year ending December 31, 2000, Delphi's average growth rate for the companies in its portfolio was 16.3 percent, while Standard & Poor's 500-stock index grew at 15.5 percent.

"The thing is that we are buying these companies at a significant discount as to price-to-book and P/E to the S&P, and our companies grow," he said.

There is one area of the market that Black avoids—or, rather, has no interest in: companies that practice what he calls "financial engineering."

"Take, for example, IBM. The company has done a pretty good job for [CEO] Lou Gerstner in increasing his wealth, and he has gotten the stock to go up, but the compound growth rate and revenues were just 3.85 percent in the year ending December 31, 2000. That doesn't impress me," he says. "It is not even [the rate of] inflation."

He continued, "We also have no interest in companies that make their I/B/E/S estimates. That is absolute nonsense. It is not important if they make 41 cents or 42 cents; it's just crap. You need to have companies that grow."

Often Black uses Benjamin Graham's concept of a margin of safety, so whenever he looks at a company he believes he has an obligation to his clients to buy it at a conservative valuation.

"If you are buying, for example, a real estate investment trust, you don't look at the price of the building next door. That is totally nonsensical. You take the free-and-clear return, which is the actual rent roll minus the operating expense, and put a cap rate on it of, say, 8.5 percent; you pull out all of the debt; and you buy it at a discount to whatever the number is," he said. "It has nothing to do with whether somebody in the neighborhood sells at 12 times income or this one is at 10. You really have to look at it just like a real estate developer pencils in a free-and-clear return and values a building for purposes of a bank loan."

Black also likes to own companies that generate free cash. For every nonfinancial company, such as a manufacturer or a service business, he does what he calls a free cash flow analysis.

"What we do is take the net income from operations, net of any divestitures, any nonrecurring items. We add in depreciation, amortization, and any deferred taxes; those are the operating sources. Then we look at the operating applications, which are the gross plant and equipment and the working capital accounts, and we like to see if [the business] is generating cash," he said. "A Walt Disney, for example, generates almost $2 billion a year, Gannett Company over a billion, and Lee Enterprises around $70 million; a little company like the Eastern Company in Naugatuck, Connecticut, that nobody has ever heard of generates a couple million in free cash. Most of the tech companies we own have bulletproof balance sheets, but they generate free cash. That is the idea, because generating cash gives you financial flexibility." By bulletproof balance sheets, Black means that the companies are real businesses backed up by real numbers.

Black believes that companies that generate free cash can live to fight another day when hard times come, while those that don't have nowhere to go.

"Look at technology, where there are short product life cycles and you have a lot of new developments. But if the cycle drops down, as it has for the last few quarters, and you don't have an all-cash balance sheet, you are done," he said.

"Another reason that we like excess cash generation is that if the stock is reasonably priced, management can go out and buy back shares," he said. "Look at a company like the Washington Post Company, which everybody knows and I have owned for 20 years. They have less than 10 million shares outstanding, because they take their excess cash and buy back the shares. It is a smart way of doing things."

While cash is something Black likes, debt is something he tries to avoid. Over 40 percent of the stocks in the portfolios have no debt or have more cash than debt.

"Companies that are vulnerable to technological change, competition, or short product life cycles are ones that can't afford to have debt," he said. "The types of businesses that you can allow to have debt are media companies like Gannett. It goes out and buys Central Newspapers and then goes out and buys an English newspaper company, and the debt it takes on to make purchases can be knocked down in a couple of years because the company generates so much free cash. For companies like Coca-Cola bottlers [Coca-Cola Enterprises] or Pepsi Bottling Group, it is fine for them to add incremental franchises, because the ongoing business generates cash."

Black said that the kinds of businesses he avoids are those that can fluctuate dramatically—energy, for example. One minute oil can sell for $85 a barrel and the next minute for

$15. Heavily leveraged companies might not make it, he believes, if they have to deal with this type of volatility.

Nevertheless, one stock that Black liked at the time we met was Vintage Petroleum, because it was trading near its lows, had a good business model, and, most important, had a huge margin of safety.

"If you back out all the debt and deferred taxes, you get a price of about $37 per share. The stock is selling at $15; against a breakup value of $37, it is selling at 40 cents on the knockdown value," he said.

At the time Black also liked some of the medium-sized newspaper companies. He believes good media franchises go out at 15 times enterprise value or more, so when he sees that he can buy Gannett Company, Inc. or the McClatchy Company or Lee Enterprises, Inc. at eight times enterprise value, he sees the companies as money machines. Although advertising revenue was down and business was not as robust as it had been, on a takeover basis the companies were selling at 50 or 60 cents on the knockdown value, which provides a solid margin of safety.

"It is not good enough to go out and buy a consumer products company with a 20 P/E that is at four times book [value], because a 20 P/E is a full takeover multiple and there is no book value to hold it in," he said. "The same thing applies to technology companies. In truth, we buy most of our tech companies when they are close to tangible value. I mean, it makes no sense to buy a company that is at $40 per share that used to sell at $100 that they think is going to earn $2 two years from now, which is a 20 P/E at six times book."

He owned shares in some technology companies when we met that he admitted were not for the weak of heart. Still, he believed that they were good businesses worth owning because they were trading near or below book value.

"Look at BTU International. The stock is down to about $3.80, the book is at $4.50, they have $3 million in debt with $10 million in cash, and they are the largest manufacturer of thermal processing machines for printer circuit boards. If you have a time horizon of more than a picosecond, and assuming they can stay the course, it is cheap because they are selling below tangible book value," he said. "Part of what we have to do here is buy at a discount to a conservative breakup value."

Black also looks at the company's accounting practices—the more conservative the better. He's quite aware that what you see is not always what you get.

"Often when people look at insurance companies, they don't look to see if there is redundancy or if it is underreserved consistently, or look at the loss-and-adjustment table," he said.

"For example, Hartford Insurance came to town earlier in the year for a deal. At the meeting people asked the normal questions. I had looked at their loss-and-adjustment table and reserve and cash-flow statements," he continued. "I didn't embarrass the manager in front of everybody, but I went up to him after and said, 'Look, you are pushing hard in the annuity business, but it looks to me like you are hemorrhaging free cash in order to grow the business.' The guy looked at me and said, 'You are not wrong.' "

Later in the year, when the St. Paul Companies, also an insurance firm, came to town, Black met with management and told them that it looked as though they also were generating negative free cash. Management told him that he was right and explained that the problem was caused by lines that were paying claims but were no longer taking premiums.

When it comes to banks, Black looks only at those that are fully reserved against nonperforming assets and other real estate owned. Wells Fargo & Company, for example, has three times reserves against nonperformers, and North Fork Bancorp has five times reserves.

"It is not good enough to have a bank that's provision is a million or two million and a quarter, even if it is a small regional and the coverage of its nonperforming assets is about one to one," he said. "These guys are sort of fooling around with reserves to make earnings."

To prove his point, he looks at Cisco Systems, Inc. The company had a straight-up record until the technology sector was hammered and then wrote down $3 billion of inventory.

"To me it is a little suspicious," he said. "Suddenly, when things aren't doing so well, they say, 'Oh, by the way, we have $3 billion in lousy inventory.' It means that they were fudging the earnings all along. Cisco is just one example of many, and I won't buy stocks like that. I have a long memory for people that play with the earnings."

Once a company meets Black's quantitative requirements, he moves on to qualitative factors. In every case, he or someone on his team speaks to the management of the companies he is interested in.

"I don't care who owns the company and what its track record is, we won't buy just because somebody else owns it. We need to call on the management, study the 10-K and 10-Q, and learn the business," he said. "The most important thing we assess is management integrity. We want to own companies that employ people that are honest, who will tell us where the strengths and weaknesses are."

One of Black's favorite examples of a company whose management had integrity is Ogilvy & Mather, the large advertising agency. Delphi owned about 3.5 percent of the company before a conglomerate took it over. Once a year, he would meet with management for lunch at Locke-Ober, a restaurant on Winter Place in the heart of Boston's financial district, to discuss the business. "Bill Phillip would come to town and tell me what all the problems were while we ate," he said. "I liked that.

"Another one that comes to mind," he continued, "is First Tennessee, the Memphis-based bank. Ron Terry used to come to town once or twice a year, and before he would take his coat off he would tell me every bad loan he made in the quarter and how he planned on improving things. We like people who are up-front with us."

Just before we met, Black took a trip to visit companies in Silicon Valley, in particular Applied Materials, Inc. He met with an old friend at the company, who told him that a lot of people may say that a turn in the technology sector is coming, but "we are the biggest on the front end, and we do not see that a turn will come until July or August of 2002."

Black likes to deal with managers who can articulate their sense of strategy, how they differentiate their product, and the competitive advantages and disadvantages of the business.

"This way of thinking is very much akin to a class called Business Policy Strategy that I had in my second year at the Harvard Business School. It taught us how to understand what makes for success in the business," he said.

The purpose of the last question that Black asks is to determine if the company has goal-orientated planning in place.

"We don't expect companies to bring in management consultants. What we want is for them to be able to communicate to us where the company is going," he said. "If we ask them where the growth in revenue is going to come from, we want them to be able to articulate it to us and for it to make sense.

"Then we have to go through the financial stuff: What's an

optimal capital structure? We look at the debt/equity ratio. What kinds of returns on capital are they getting, and what are the margins?" he continued. "You take them through these things and test their assumptions based on what they have done in the past. If a company says they are going to grow at 15 percent, which is to double every five years, and we point out that on a smaller base they have grown at only 7 or 8 percent annually, we want to know what makes them think they can achieve this goal."

When it comes to manufacturing companies, Black likes to get involved in the production process. He talks to management about things like the people on the shop floor and where they have bottlenecks in the production process.

"People always take production for granted; you never see a sell-side report talking about manufacturing and flow until something goes wrong," he said. "In many cases I—or if I take analysts, we—go out on the plant floor to see what the heck is going on. I want to understand that when somebody says that they have a cluster tool with wafer etch, I want to understand what they are talking about." (A few years ago, Black actually had Lam Research Corporation take him out in front of a cluster tool with wafer etch in a clean room so he could understand the process.)

"I want to understand if it is a job shop, if it is an assembly line, or if it is partial customization," he continued. "I want to know how they manufacture the product and understand the work flow."

But regardless of how the company functions or will function, Black said the most important thing is people.

"I want to know if they have homegrown management, if they look outside, where they come from, and how they are compensated," he said. "One of the things we are really strict on is people getting overpaid by either getting new options rewritten after the stock tanks or getting it in salary.

"The idea that someone can walk into a business and be handed two million shares of stock for doing absolutely nothing does not really appeal to me," he continued. "Look at Lou Gerstner, who has made four or five hundred million dollars personally and the company [IBM] has had nominal growth, compared to someone like Andy Grove of Intel or Warren Buffett, who take nominal salaries and have built the companies that have double-digit growth."

While names like the Microsoft Corporation or Merck & Company, Inc. or Pfizer, Inc. might seem to match Black's criteria, he would never own them. Instead he looks for companies that offer a high-earning power play, companies that have a high return on equity year in and year out. One example Black used to illustrate his point was Jack-in-the-Box, Inc. The fast-food company has earned more than 29 percent on book value for the past five years, and it has had one break in earnings in five years.

"We bought the stock down at $24 or $25, and we think that they are going to earn $2.65 next year, which would make it a 9 P/E. Our cutoff for companies with consistent earnings, even if it was Microsoft, is 12.9 P/E. We don't pay any more than 12.9 times on our own internal estimated earnings from our own models.

"I don't care what the company is; if it does not sell just below the 13-multiple cusp, we are not interested," he continued. "This is a built-in mechanism for the margin of safety, because when you don't overpay P/E-wise, you are not going to get killed."

This saved him from taking significant losses when the Internet and technology sectors collapsed. Black likes to say that he had four Internet stocks: Goldman Sachs, Morgan Stanley, Heidrick & Struggles International, Inc., and Information Holdings. He sums up his theory on Internet stocks with a baseball analogy: "We are not here to chase fastballs high up in the strike zone!"

One of the things Black believes gives him an edge is that he is willing to look at all sorts of obscure companies. Some of his companies have market caps as low as $40 million.

"Look at a company like Eastern Company; it has earned 20 percent on book for the past three years, and yet nobody loves the company, and I don't understand why," he said. "It makes no difference to us; we own tons of small, little companies that are all very good.

"We are not afraid; we try to be intellectually inquisitive. The day that we have to sit back and rely on sell-side analysts calling us is the day that Delphi is going to close," he continued. "Our thing is to mathematically screen companies. We use all of the tools available to us to get as much information as possible to make good decisions, and everything is fair game to us. We are not afraid to think independently. When it looks the bleakest, we will step into companies that have solid balance sheets and purchase the stocks in advance of the turn."

The Delphi portfolios consist of 60 to 65 stocks, and while they are diversified by name they are concentrated by industry. Historically, 20 percent of the firm's assets have been in media stocks because, according to Black, the next best thing to robbing a bank is to own a good television station, newspaper, or cable network.

He has also spent a lot of time investing in the financial services sector, in particular regional banks, which he finds to be nuts-and-bolts operations, simple but elegant.

Black said that while he would like to be able to take credit for creating his investment style, he has very much based it on that of Buffett and a friend of Buffett's, William Ruane of Ruane, Cuniff & Co. Ruane told him that the way to be successful was to buy companies with low price-to-earnings ratios and high returns on equity.

"I did exactly that and it makes sense, because when you find a good business that you can buy on the cheap, you don't have the risk," he said. "It lets you sleep at night."

He doesn't do it alone, however. He has a solid team to help him that he works very hard to train. He admits that a lot of people have passed through the firm, but he believes it is because they recognize the training they get.

"My best success comes from people right out of college, not business school, who have no predispositions, whom I can teach all about business and most importantly to think," he said. "I work my people very hard, but they really learn the discipline. They eat, sleep, and drink value investing."

Black believes more people don't invest the way he does because it isn't very exciting.

"You can't sit at a cocktail party and say, 'I own this company and it is a 12 percent grower that generates free cash.' It is not very exciting, and people want instant gratification," he said. "This is why they had all those initial public offerings with no earnings and no revenues that went from $20 to $100 in the same day and they thought they knew something. On top of that, you really have to work at it, and you may know the strategy, but you have to find the companies to fit the strategy—and people are lazy.

"What I do for a living is to literally pick through the flawed merchandise. I need to know when I go through the racks at Filene's Basement whether I am getting my wife an

Armani dress that has been marked down from $400 to $100 or some polyester [dress] that has been marked down," he continued. "It is a tough thing, and it is not that interesting to many people. People want excitement, and we are not interested in excitement; we are interested in making money for our clients over time."

And he has performed. Since 1984 Delphi's portfolios are up 3,615 percent, compared to the S&P, which is up around 2,300 percent. Black sums it all up with another baseball analogy, saying that he is like Tony Gwynn and Wade Boggs. "I probably will never hit in home run derbies like Sammy Sosa or Barry Bonds, but if you want guys that can hit .340 or .350 over a lifetime and score some runs, that is what we are trying to do."

"One of the best compliments that I ever got was from one of the investment professionals at Sunkist, who called me the Tony Gwynn of investing," he said. "We don't panic, we play under control, and we just try to buy good businesses."

★ ★ ★

What I Think . . .

While some of you might have heard of Scott Black before you picked up this book, I am sure most of you hadn't. It is amazing that more people don't invest with this manager. At the time of this writing, the Delphi mutual fund managed less than $50 million.

The reason why it isn't over $500 million is simple: Black doesn't seem to believe in marketing and is more interested in posting strong returns than in doing road shows to raise assets. He is content with his institutional business and the relatively small number of retail accounts. Some may call it shortsighted, but I think it is professional. There is nothing wrong with waiting for people to find you instead of trying to find people.

Mary Lisanti

Mary Lisanti is considered by most fund watchers to be one of the best growth fund managers of all time. For more than nine years, regardless of market cap, Lisanti and her team continue to prove time and again that they are at the top of their game.

Lisanti began her career on Wall Street as an analyst after graduating from Princeton University with a degree in English.

"I got out of school in the late 1970s, and there were no jobs in the city for English majors. So I looked for a position where I could use my writing skills and went to work for another Princeton grad, who thought that working on Wall Street would be good for me," she said. "After talking to some people and working for a few months, I decided I liked the research side of the business. It reminded me of writing my thesis, because, just like that project, every research had a conclusion."

She took a job as a junior analyst at E. F. Hutton and spent the next few years learning how to analyze companies and look at the markets.

"I heard that Hutton was starting a junior analyst program and called the director of research. He asked me what I wanted to do. I said I wanted to write like Hemingway, and he said, 'You're hired,'" she said. "I started in the program and was trained how to analyze companies, and from there it just sort of stuck—I basically lucked into it and fell in love with it."

Since then she has worked at a number of Wall Street's best-known firms, including the former Bankers Trust and Strong Capital Management. Now she is executive vice president and chief investment officer of domestic equities at ING Pilgrim Investments Inc.

She not only oversees all the firm's U.S.-based mutual funds but also heads the group that manages over $7 billion in the firm's small-, mid-, and large-cap growth mutual funds.

"As chief investment officer, my role is to guide the overall investment strategy of the firm for both the internally managed products and the products that are subadvised," she said. "Overseeing basically means that I make sure they do everything that they say that they are going to do. I understand their investment process and make sure they have an adequate amount of resources to manage the portfolios. However, my primary role is to be the thought leader for all of our investment products."

Lisanti said she tries to get people to think about all aspects of the market in order to understand how political and economic issues are going to affect the portfolios that they manage.

"The idea is to look not just at what is going on in the economy but also to think about stock investing in the context of what is going on now and what we think will happen in the future," she said, "and to come up with investment ideas and a plan that will let us capitalize on current and future events."

When we met, which was just after the October 2001 Federal Open Market Committee meeting, Lisanti was working with her financial services managers on a strategy for the sector for when interest rates stop going down.

"Eventually interest rates will stop falling, and when they do we will not be able to make the trade out in a day, so we want to be prepared for it and act accordingly," she said. "Everybody is going to say that you should trade out of these sorts of banks into these sorts of banks, so I want them to be thinking about it six months ahead of time. If they don't start doing it before the last interest rate cut becomes effective, they will get caught in a squeeze and the portfolio will suffer.

"The idea is to get people to start thinking on a broad basis, proactively," she continued. "We need to be thinking about what is going on in the world, where things are going, and what is happening, so that we can not only understand companies in the context of the stock but also understand what the market has already priced into it."

From a chief investment officer's viewpoint, what Lisanti looks at is how the portfolio managers in her group actually do their work, which comes down to understanding how the people are analyzing stocks.

Because she leads an investment team as well, she also has to focus on carrying out the investment strategy of her portfolios. They consist of large-, mid-, and small-cap funds and an all-cap fund, which is sort of a hybrid of the three. In this capacity, she is directly responsible for managing just over $7 billion.

Her team comprises 12 professionals, four of whom are sector heads, plus a value specialist, while the remaining seven are analysts and junior analysts.

"The sector heads focus on technology, health care and consumer, and business, industrial and energy across all market caps," she said. "I don't think you can look at small-cap companies and make an educated decision about a company unless you know what everyone in the sector is doing.

"I don't see how anyone can invest in a small networking company unless they know what Cisco is doing, and I don't know how anyone can invest in Cisco if they don't know what the small networking company is doing," she continued. "To me, these divisions are sort of silly, and I think that it hurts the investment process, so we look at the entire sector and don't focus on one sort of asset class."

The team works to come up with investment ideas for all the portfolios. Working together, she believes, is better than if each focused on one area and came up with ideas separately.

For the most part, each of the firm's growth portfolios looks at 200 to 250 names and runs with about 100 positions. Often there is some overlap between the funds, although during the market slide of 2000 and 2001 the large-cap fund was more concentrated than the others, because the team couldn't find good investment opportunities for it.

"It is very hard as a growth investor to find more than 30 or 40 names that will fit in a large-cap portfolio," she said. "Right now everything is small- and mid-cap, and most of the ones that have gone from large- to small- or mid-cap have done so for a very specific reason: They belonged there in the first place and the market overpriced them."

Lisanti said that the small-cap fund is less concentrated than the others, because liquidity is much more of an issue with small caps. She is not "a big believer" of taking outsized risk just to juice up returns.

"We want to make sure that we do not own too much of a stock, so that if there is a problem, we don't get caught in a liquidity crunch," she said.

The overall investment process for the funds is a combination of top-down and bottom-up analysis. She has used the basic principle for more than nine years, since her days at Bankers Trust.

The core of her team is people who have been with her since her time there. They work with the newer members to educate them about their investment approach as well as to take ideas from them on how to improve it.

"I developed the process while I was a sell-side analyst," she said. "When I talked to people, it became clear that everybody seemed to manage money one of two ways—either from a pure top-down perspective or from a pure bottom-up perspective. Either way, they inevitably ended up in trouble, because the top-down people didn't know the details of companies, and the bottom-up people would sometimes make sector bets that they did not know they were making."

Just so everyone is clear, a top-down strategy entails analysis that first looks at the economy, then selects an industry, and finally picks an individual stock, based on economic, political, and sociological trends.

"We try to think about what is going to happen in the context of the world—where we want to be—and not just stick with what we are comfortable with, but push out to other things to make sure we are complete in our analysis," she said.

Lisanti defines the bottom-up side of the analysis as the actual work of finding investment opportunities. Once the team comes up with an analysis, they then have to find investments that fit it.

"It can be a great concept, but you have to know if the company can execute; [you have to] understand the business model and the strength of management's ability," she said. "It is the companies that either have a view of what they bring to the world or have a very specific view of the value-added in whatever industry they happen to be in that we believe over time are the most successful.

"You can sit down and talk to the guy who runs Lear Industries, and he would have told you when he came public exactly where the company was going," she continued. "As he has executed on the strategy, in some years the stock did well and in some years it did not, but overall the company has done very well. That is the sort of thing we want to get a sense of. If you invest in a company that really has no sense about who they are and where they are going, the minute they hit hard times, they are going to blow."

Lisanti said that most people forget how hard it is to build good companies. And while she has not forgotten that, most of the stocks that her funds own start with a minimum of 15 percent earnings growth and eventually turn into 20 percent to 30 percent growers.

"It is incredibly hard to maintain consistent earnings growth. In order to do it, everybody really needs to be marching to the same drummer," she said. "That is why the judgment of the top people really comes into play. If the top layer of the company is not strong, then the company will not march in step and really won't be able to grow."

By combining approaches, Lisanti believes that she is able to find ideas and execute on them more effectively than her peers. In particular, she believes that this strategy will help guide the funds successfully through the market volatility in the wake of the World Trade Center disaster.

"It is the first time in 12 years that we are combining monetary stimulus and fiscal stimulus, so what I have to do is go back in my mind to the 1980s and 1970s and remember how the world looked in order to have some sense of what will happen," she said. "We really want to try to have a view of how the world will look that is different from the consensus view. That ends up helping us, regardless of the level of volatility in the market."

As chief investment officer, Lisanti does most of the work to determine the economic outlook for the firm and then, with her team, structures the portfolios based on various themes.

"As growth investors, we want to look at the way the world is going to be, because we are investing in companies on what they are going to be, not on what they are today. Therefore we like to make some assumptions about how the world is going to look and try to see what makes sense," she said. "A large part of any good investment project is common sense and logic. If you sort of lay out your investment thinking as clearly as possible and look at all the permutations of it, then you will be able to see if there are any holes in the logic."

For example, if she is going to invest in a retail company, she realizes that she is making a number of assumptions, not just about the economy, but about a raft of other things: inventory control, cotton prices, currency fluctuation, and political instability in countries where clothing is made.

"If we don't make connections between our companies and all the aspects of the markets that they touch, then we will end up lost and wasting a lot of time," she said. "There is so much information today that a lot of what we have to do is to filter out what is not important.

"We have to sort out all of this material and decide what matters. Otherwise we just end up reacting rather than being thoughtful about what we are doing," she continued. "The whole idea is to have some framework around which we hang the portfolio so we can look at and understand the reasons behind its structure."

Lisanti said that many growth managers buy companies

that look secular but really are cyclical. The minute the economy changes, the companies go from being secular to being cyclical, and the managers are crushed.

"There are very few companies that are secular growth stocks, and people get them confused and really can't find them," she said. "You have to understand what they are doing and how they are doing it.

"Microsoft for a long time was a true secular growth story, because it understood the implications of the move to personal computers in the workforce, so it dominated the operating system market. That ideally is what we are looking for," she continued. "The problem is we can't always find them. There is nothing wrong with owning a cyclical company, but you'd better know that it is cyclical."

Lisanti said that while she does not invest with a 10-year horizon, she does believe that thinking about the next 10 years allows her to come up with some of her most creative ideas.

"We all spent about six years wandering around the wilderness in the 1980s thinking about technology. They were lean and mean times," she said. "When the Gulf War came, it was clear that the technology worked and all the investments that we made paid off.

"That was the psychological trigger that forced a lot of technology investment, because up until then a lot of corporations were not too sure they wanted to do it. One chief economist even wrote an article saying the idea that technology could improve productivity was completely a myth. What no one factored in was that it takes a generation to do something in a meaningful way," she continued. "Until that sort of thing factors through to a business, it does not improve productivity, so that is the kind of thing people had forgotten about."

Lisanti said that what happened in the early 1990s was that

people who bought technology stocks ended up making great investments if—a big if—they were not shaken out of the stocks by the noise about the companies making or not making numbers.

"Just like drugs was the sector to be in in the 1980s, technology was the place to be in the 1990s," she said. "There are all sorts of things that if we can figure them out, then we have a sense at least of where we are getting potentially major secular changes and where we are just dealing with cyclical events."

When Lisanti identifies secular changes pounding a stock, she most likely will increase the fund's position in it. On the other hand, when she finds cyclical changes, she looks at the position solely as a trading stock. Then it does not matter how hot the name is or how many people on the Street follow the stock; she will not add the stock to her portfolio.

In the fall of 2001, Lisanti thought that as the recession continued the economy would turn upward and there would be very mild inflation—1 or 2 percent. She believes that a little inflation is a good thing, since it would allow companies to gain back the pricing power they lost in the technology boom.

"I don't know if it is going to happen, but if it does I want to be prepared," she said. "Part of the problem for many corporations has been that they are not getting unit growth and their prices have been going down, causing it to be very hard to manage profitability. If they are able to increase prices and gain some pricing power, they will be able to return to more significant rates of profitability.

"It is just a thesis, and when you invest in growth you are in the business of developing a series of theses and seeing if they work," she continued. "It does not mean that you commit all of your capital to the idea, but it does mean that companies that have struggled through the 1990s may have a little bit easier time in this decade."

Stocks that Lisanti puts in this category are general business and some consumer service firms, ones that unlike computer companies are not able to drive prices higher year after year while costs fall or hold steady.

"There are very few businesses like technology companies that are able to increase prices as their prices go down," she said. "So companies that have struggled with their profitability and for the most part played corporate accounting games to keep things looking good now might actually be able to do a little better."

On fiscal policy, Lisanti laughs when she hears Congress and the Bush administration say that stimulus programs will last only a year.

"Once they start doing it, they keep doing it, obviously to less of a degree, but you can't just stop a government program on a dime," she said. "Plus when people want to get reelected, what better way to do it than to spend some money on their constituents?"

Lisanti's whole investment process is based on guiding people toward what she calls "inflection points": an ever-changing list of characteristics of companies that are on their way to becoming growth companies or those that had been growth companies until they had some problem, but see their businesses as getting better and stronger and returning to significant levels of growth.

"The idea that mild inflation may go back into the economy is a major secular change, which could benefit many companies," she said. "If that happens, it will push investment, because people will believe that life will get a little easier for companies that have struggled."

To start the investment process, Lisanti and her team begin by screening a lot of databases so they can see the world as it is, not as they think it is.

"We don't want our memory of 10 or 15 years ago to color our view of today, so we look where there are improvements in profitability or return on equity or improvements from cash and where that disconnects from the stock price. That usually happens when people are not paying attention or when people think that the future will not be as good as the past," she said. "Now that we finally have confirmation that we are in a recession, everyone is convinced that we will not come out of it or that it will take a long time to come out. My question is, what do these people think we have been doing for the last 18 months?

"When people get nervous, they don't want to look past their noses. Well, we are paid to do just that," she continued. "Part of our process is to step back and not only look at the company now but also get a view of how it is going to be in six months or a year from now."

By identifying things that Lisanti believes the rest of the world has overlooked, she believes that she adds significant value for her shareholders, and in some cases she can be early to an opportunity.

Unlike some other growth fund managers who look only at the consumer, health care, financial services, and technology sectors for investment opportunities, she will look anywhere. As long as she can make a case for secular growth, she will make a case for any company that she finds.

"When the utilities deregulated, all of a sudden they were growth companies, and they did indeed grow their earnings by 70 percent and were the best-performing sector that year. So why, as a growth fund manager, would I not want to be in there?" she said. "The idea is to be able to identify something that is going to happen and get to it before everyone else does."

If she can find information about a specific industry or area of the market that indicates that the companies might experience an increased return on invested capital, then she will be there, too.

Lisanti employs a valuation discipline and a sell discipline. She does not believe in paying more than the growth rate of a company, and by doing her own numbers she can get a better understanding of what is going on than by reading a report.

"I was trained in the late 1970s on how to analyze a company by doing massive cash-flow analysis, by asking tons of questions, and by visiting with anybody related in some way to the company. In the end we would come out with a 50-page report on the company," she said. "What it taught us was how to analyze things very thoroughly."

Today Lisanti pretty much does the same analysis on a company as she did when she was starting out. Now, however, because of technology and the information flow, she is able to do it faster and more efficiently.

"In periods of growth and liquidity, you don't have to worry about balance sheets," she said. "And now for the first time in a very long time liquidity is going to be tighter and money is going to be tougher to get, and so companies with a strong balance sheet are going to win."

Lisanti thinks the environment of the fall of 2000 was saner and more rational than that of the more recent past, when companies have been performing more disparately.

"I have never seen so much evenness amongst S&P companies in terms of the rate of earnings growth," she said. "This will result in a much greater spread along the spectrum of about 7, 8, or 9 percent growth rate."

"I think of it as back to the future. Balance sheets matter, fundamentals matter, and strategy matters. Everything that really did not matter in the last five years is really going to count going forward."

★ ★ ★

What I Think . . .

When I started working on this project, I asked a number of people for names of managers whom I should include. Three of the first five said I had to talk to Mary Lisanti. I had heard of her and the work she was doing, but we'd never met. When we finally did, I understood why she was at the top of the list. Lisanti is more than a money manager; she's an economist—someone who looks at the big picture and all that is in it. She looks at the whole market like a jigsaw puzzle and uses companies and their ideas as the pieces.

Her approach to investing is different from many of the others profiled in these pages. She doesn't accept the gospel of Warren Buffett, but instead follows her own path. I think that's what gives her her edge. That and another thing: People believe in her.

Nothing illustrates this more clearly than the fact that most of her team has been with her for more than 10 years. There is something about the way her leadership, determination, and ability have made these people stick around so long. They are three qualities that make for one good money manager.

Christopher Browne

Since the 1920s, Tweedy, Browne Company LLC has separated itself from the rest of Wall Street by exploiting unique niches in the marketplace. Unlike most firms that try to be all things to all people, over the years Tweedy has basically decided to do one thing and one thing only—and to be very good at it.

Today the firm still follows one investment strategy that is based on "the concepts of intrinsic value and margin of safety as conceived and practiced by Benjamin Graham." It oversees more than $7 billion, both in separate accounts and in two no-load mutual funds.

"We have always tried to find an area where we would not have much competition," said Christopher Browne, one of the firm's managing directors and son of one of the firm's early principals, who focuses on investing in international small-cap stocks.

The business began in the 1920s as a brokerage firm specializing in companies with limited stock marketability because they had few outside shareholders. "In some cases the companies had 50 or 150 outside shareholders, and Forrest Tweedy would go to the annual meetings, get the names of shareholders, and then send them postcards to let them know that there was a market for their stock if they wanted to sell it or to buy more," Browne said. "He basically became a market maker for these closely held, inactively traded companies when other firms were ignoring them."

In the early 1930s, as the business grew, Tweedy developed a relationship with Ben Graham. Graham was looking for cheap stocks, and the firm not only had information on the illiquid companies but was also making markets in them. It was a natural fit for the two to do business together.

"All of the inactively traded stocks that Tweedy was making markets in traded at a significant discount to book value, making them real cheap. Graham liked cheap stocks," Browne said.

In 1945 Tweedy expanded and added two partners, Browne's father, Howard, and Joe Reilly, and it became known as Tweedy, Browne & Reilly. One of the first things the company did was to move its offices next to Graham's. The thinking was that the closer their offices were, the more business the firms would do with each other.

The firm continued being market makers for "cheap bargain-basement stocks" for some time, becoming the only market for some companies, and in turn making its niche on Wall Street even more comfortable.

In the late 1950s Graham decided to retire. Initially he offered the business to two of the people who worked for him, Warren Buffett and Tom Knapp. Both Buffett and Knapp had taken Graham's course at Columbia University in security analysis and had been at his firm for some time. Buffett declined, deciding instead to move back to Omaha, where the rest, as they say, is history. Knapp decided to go to work for Tweedy, and the firm became known as Tweedy, Browne & Knapp.

"In 1957, Tweedy retired. The principals believed that they always needed at least three partners to insure proper coverage, so when Forest decided to retire, [the remaining partners] thought that it was a natural fit to ask Knapp to come work at the firm," Browne said. "The thing was that Tom was not interested in becoming a broker. He wanted to continue being an investor, as he had been working for Graham. He wanted to basically buy the stocks and hold them."

So Knapp joined the firm and the firm began its transition

from broker to money manager. While Knapp was focusing on investments and establishing a track record, the rest of the firm continued as a broker, making markets for thinly traded stocks.

"These were not stocks that you would call great companies," Browne said. "These were stocks that were trading at one-third or two-thirds of book. Remember, this was back when people were buying companies like Fownes Gloves and coal mines, which were selling at two-thirds net current assets. It was before the better business era."

While Knapp was building the money management business, Browne's father and Walter Schloss, another partner, started offering stocks to Buffett.

"After one of the first trades Warren executed with my father, Buffett called up Walter and said, 'This guy Howard Browne is one of the stupidest people I have ever met.' Walter asked why, and Buffett replied, 'Well, who in their right mind would sell you stocks that are that cheap?' Walter explained, 'Well, they can't afford to buy them all themselves so they spread it around.' From that point on a relationship developed, and my father became Warren's sort of principal broker in the 1960s."

Tweedy, Browne was the brokerage that sold Buffett most of his Berkshire Hathaway stock. Because Buffett had a rule that his brokers could not buy anything he was buying, the firm did not get to buy stock in any of the same companies as Buffett. In those days Berkshire was trading under $20 a share; in October 2001, it was trading at just under $75,000 a share.

In the late 1960s Reilly decided to retire from the firm. (He started working with Knapp managing the firm's portfolio, which at the time had over 600 names in it. Even though he was retired, Reilly continued to come to the office every day until his death in 1992.)

Again looking for a third partner, the firm found Ed Anderson.

Anderson had been a nuclear physicist with the Atomic Energy Commission. He developed an interest in investing and started an investment club that bought stocks that were trading at two-thirds net current assets. In 1965, he decided to leave the AEC and took a job working with Charlie Munger at his investment partnership in California, but by 1968 he'd decided to come back East. When he returned to New York, he brought his investment partnership along, marking the first time Tweedy, Browne was managing money for clients outside the firm.

So from that point on Tweedy, Browne & Knapp was a limited partnership, pouring the cement that would become the foundation of one of the best global value managers of all time.

Strengthening the money management arm led to the firm being split into one entity that focused on money management and another that focused on brokerage. When Chris Browne joined the firm, it really began to move fully into money management.

In the summer of 1968, on the advice of a friend, Browne joined the Army Reserve. He made it through the first semester of his senior year at the University of Pennsylvania without being called up, but was ordered in for his six months' active duty training before the second semester started in 1969. When he got out of the Army in June, he came to New York and, after a night of which he has "no recollection of what happened," ended up in the city with no money.

"I went down to the office to borrow five bucks from my father to take the train home," he said. "And when I got there, I met Ed Anderson and we started chatting and, as a polite kid, I sat down and sort of nodded my head as he talked. At the end of the conversation, he asked what I was going to do this summer. I said I didn't know, and he said I should work at the firm, and I said, 'Okay, that sounds like a good idea.'"

He continued, "My father was surprised that I was going to work in the office. When I told him, though, that I had to go to reserve meetings once a month and therefore had to stay in the area, we both sort of agreed that it would be a good thing to do."

So Browne joined the firm and started working with Anderson to learn how to find stocks that met his criteria for the portfolio. During the summer the University of Pennsylvania wrote Browne, saying that it had changed its requirements and that he now had enough credits to graduate.

"Suddenly I did not have to go back to school. I went to my father and Ed and asked if I could work for a year at the firm and then I would go to business school," he said. "They said sure, and that was it. I ended up never going to business school; I just stayed working at the firm."

Browne said that he decided against business school after a discussion with his brother Tony, who had recently graduated from Harvard Business School and was working at a hedge fund.

"Tony told me that the only reason to go to business school was to get a job on Wall Street, and since I already had one, why go? And so I did not go," he said.

Now, more than 30 years later, Browne is still at the firm, as one of its five managing directors.

Tweedy, Browne is often singled out as one of the best value management firms of all time. Both its mutual funds continue to put up solid investment performance and have extremely long records of success. While most people believe that past performance does not guarantee future results, it is hard to use that argument about Tweedy, Browne.

Browne began his career by starting each day posting the trades from the day before and taking lunch orders. Eventually he started working closely with Anderson on various projects that provided him with the fundamentals of the firm's investment strategy.

"Ed would hand me a copy of a bank directory and the national register from the Quotation Bureau and would tell me to pick a state and look up the banks," he said. "When I found banks that had publicly traded stocks, I would then compute the book value of the company. If the bid price was two-thirds of the book value I would submit a bid, so that when the pink sheets next came out we would be in there with a bid."

Browne said he did this exercise for 48 states, and Tweedy, Browne ended up owning "little bits and pieces" of banks all around the country.

Along with working the books, he would work with the Standard & Poor's *Digest*, trying to compute net current assets of thinly traded companies. If the results met Ed's investment criteria, Browne would submit bids for those stocks, as well.

"The work was sort of brainless, but it was how research was done at Tweedy in those days," he said. "Today we pretty much do the same thing, except we use computers to crunch the numbers."

In the early 1970s two things happened that really set the firm on the path of focusing on money management. The first was a closed-end fund that had owned a lot of the tech bubble names that had tanked during the 1973 to 1974 bear market.

Although the fund had a net asset value of $5 a share, it was trading at $3.

"We started buying the fund, and then we came across some other people who were buying the fund. We tried to come up with a plan so that we could work together, but it did not work out. So we ended up buying them out, and finally we pushed out the management and took control," he said. "When we got control, we liquidated the portfolio and bought all of our own stocks and in the process became a registered investment adviser."

The other thing that happened was the firm's move away from the clearing-and-settlement side of the business. During the early and mid-1970s as new discount firms were emerging, Tweedy, Browne started working with Discount Brokerage Corporation.

"Our back office was losing money, and we needed to find a way to stem the losses. We decided to get out of that part of the business and focus on money management," he said. "The idea was that if we could get 10 million [dollars' worth] in assets under management, we would basically be out of the red forever.

"When Discount Brokerage Corporation opened their door they were the first firm like it to be able to self-clear, and they did from our office," he continued. "We started to focus on the money management side and let them focus on the back office side."

One of the unique things that the partners believed that they had going for them was the fact that Knapp had kept track of the investment record since his arrival in 1958. By having the data to compute the track record, they believed they could build a solid business, so they started marketing themselves as long-term money managers.

"John Spears joined the firm around the same time. He had been working with Bill Berger of the Berger Funds and on the side was managing a small partnership with a few hundred thousand in it that he ran with the same Ben Graham principles as we ran our money," he said. "So the two of us started focusing on the investment adviser business and realized that the process worked, so all we needed to do was to find clients."

The first thing Browne did was to buy a list of people who had invested in tax shelters. They mailed a letter to everybody on the list and got only one response, from the partner who ran the trust and estates department at a large New York law firm. The partners thought they had it made, since once they explained how they did things and showed him the record, they believed he would be able refer a significant amount of business to the firm.

"He must have interviewed us five times, and every time he would come in we kept thinking he must be acting on behalf of other people—or at least, because he was so well connected, he would be able to refer us business. Well, we were wrong," he said.

After the lengthy interview process, the lawyer opened an account at the firm (its first account as a registered investment adviser) with $50,000. That was the last time they heard from him until more than a decade later, when he called to close his account.

"He'd compounded his money with us at a rate of about 23 percent for well over 10 years, and he called me one day to tell me that he was retiring and that he wanted to liquidate the account," Browne said. "I asked him if he was unhappy, and he said, 'No, but I want to put the money in municipals so I can have some income.' He never referred anyone else to us and, once he closed his account, we never got another shred of business out of him."

During this period Browne and Spears were struggling to come up with ways to find clients and to raise money. Finally they hit pay dirt when *Fortune* magazine published an article about the firm. From that point on, they were really in the money management business.

"A small article appeared in the magazine as one of those boxes inside the main story, and once it appeared, the phone started ringing off the hook," Browne said. "All of a sudden people started finding us and we started attracting clients and their assets."

Around the time of the *Fortune* write-up, about 1976, Browne and Spears met with a partner of a large institution. They explained to him the firm's style and strategy for managing money and its plans for building that side of the business.

"The guy calls us the next day and says that he wants to open an account with us for $10 million," he said. "We told him that we would have to think about it. First of all, it was a lot of money, and, second, we thought they would come in and try to dominate the business and be a real pain. After checking them out and realizing this was not going to be the case, we accepted the $10 million and today we still have the account."

The firm derives its approach to money management from Graham, emphasizing the preservation of capital while seeking a "satisfactory rate" of return. Browne said the basis for the style is the idea that every publicly traded company's stock has a two-tier price structure. The first is the stock market value, the most recent price at which shares traded on the open market. The second is the intrinsic value, which includes the book value, current net asset value, earnings value, and private market value.

The firm's research focuses on determining the intrinsic value.

"We use fundamental principles of balance sheet and income statement analysis and a knowledge of understanding actual corporate mergers, acquisitions, and liquidations to form the core of this research," Browne said. "From a list of more than 20,000 publicly traded corporations around the world, we research and select for investment those stocks that sell at 50 or 60 percent of our estimate of the company's intrinsic value."

Browne said the firm's task as an investment manager is to take advantage of fluctuations in stock prices by buying securities far below intrinsic value, and then selling them as their price approaches intrinsic value.

"To make sure that we minimize errors in the analysis of events that could adversely affect intrinsic values, we adhere to a policy of broad diversification within the portfolios, with no one position accounting for more than 3 percent to 4 percent of the portfolio's assets," he said. "Along with that, we do not allow one industry group to account for more than 15 percent to 20 percent of the portfolio's value."

In the late 1970s, Browne started looking at value stocks outside the United States, after Jim Clark, a colleague at another house, asked him for help in finding firms interested in stocks that were trading at a discount to book value. Clark wanted to establish a business where he would earn a commission on the transaction for introducing the idea to the client.

"He found this funny little stock in the Caribbean that was selling at a discount to cash, and he wanted us to help him find places for him to go with it," Browne said. "We started talking. Along with having information on a bunch of these types of stocks, he also had access to a lot of rich people. From there, we came up with the idea of setting up a partnership with people he knew from these circles that we would run side by side with our other portfolios."

Clark joined the firm, bringing with him not only the foundation for a good business but also an angle to investing that Browne and his colleagues had never thought of before.

"Prior to Jim's arrival, we always had to buy stocks that had tangible book value and tangible net current assets. He explained to us how to value a television station, which is nothing more than 10 times cash flow, and it made a lot of sense to us," Browne said. "From that point on we started looking at appraising a business, as opposed to simply putting a value on its balance sheet."

In the early 1980s the firm spent a lot of time working with leveraged buyout (LBO) firms, providing them access to its portfolios of cheap stocks.

"Basically, the formula that LBO firms were using at the time to take out these companies was to pay four and a half times earnings, plus the debt and the cash," said Browne. "And in the early 1980s you could buy almost all of corporate America with this formula."

Along with getting involved in LBOs, Tweedy, Browne also got involved with liquidators. The concept was that if a company had a division that was not making money, the division was still worth at least half of its book value. Clark came up with this idea because of a section in the tax code that allowed a company to take a write-off if it gave its assets away. In those days the tax rate was 50 percent; therefore the unprofitable division was worth at least half of its book value.

"So we started looking for opportunities where the companies looked like they were ready for a takeover or liquidation, slowly transiting out of straight discount to book value research," Browne said.

Browne and Spears developed the international aspect of the business in the early and mid-1980s when they met a guy who had worked with Graham. He told them to look at Japanese insurance companies, the stocks of which, he said, were selling at a third of book value.

"We said, 'Great!' and started to look into the companies and found that they were all trading at book. We couldn't figure out what the guy was talking about or what we were missing," he said.

The guy explained to Spears that the prices of the companies were based on the price of their securities portfolios at cost, but that when the portfolios were priced at the market, they were trading at a third of book value. Spears asked how he could find out the information. The guy told him that the companies filed the necessary information with the stock exchange, the only problem being that it was written in Japanese.

"We had someone go into the exchange, get the information, translate it, and, sure enough, the guy was right and the stocks were trading at a third of book," Browne said. "It has always been better to be lucky rather than smart, and a short time later the exchanges changed the filing requirements, and now the companies were submitting the data in both English and Japanese."

With Japanese markets now available to all, Browne and his colleagues began to set their sights on other regions of the world for investment opportunities. One of the problems they found was that because of the lack of data it was very hard to make investment decisions.

Through a relationship with an investment banker in Britain, they found a number of databases that purported to have the necessary information but actually didn't. It was not until the early 1990s that they found one that had what they needed and really began to explore opportunities in other countries.

"We went to our investment banker friend and told him that now we had the tools to manage money with international stocks, and we set up a fund with him," Browne said. "It turned out to be basically shooting fish in a barrel. In those days, Europe was in the tank, stocks were at ridiculously low valuations, and all we had to do was figure out the accounting issues and go from there."

Today Browne takes the same approach to investing outside the United States as he does when investing in U.S. stocks. By looking at stocks outside the United States, the firm both expands its investment horizon and diversifies its risk by investing in economies that are not correlated with the U.S. stock market.

What Browne found overseas was that instead of the accounting issues being a minefield, as he expected, they turned out to be a treasure hunt.

"A lot of European accounting is designed to hide assets and hide earnings. They always want to understate everything," he said. "So once we got through it, all we had to do was deal with the currency issues, and from there we were set.

"Throughout the years, the firm has honed its skills in understanding foreign business practices and the different reporting and accounting procedures used by non-U.S. companies," he continued. "On the firm's entire investment team, we have capabilities in six languages, including English, and we maintain an office in London to facilitate research and on-site access to companies."

The bulk of the investment process and portfolio construction is based on a strict bottom-up research approach, focused entirely on stock-by-stock valuation analysis.

"The portfolios are diversified by country, sector, and issue, and consist primarily of equity securities in developed markets," Browne said. "The companies have a range in market capitalization with significant exposure to small- and medium-cap companies, as well as some micro-caps."

The firm does not try to predict the movement in currencies. "We believe that currency fluctuations are often more extreme than stock market fluctuations and, from our perspective, completely unpredictable," he said.

To eliminate the risk, Browne hedges the portfolio's foreign currency exposure back to the U.S. dollar.

"Our own research, as well as that of other academics, suggests that this can be done over long periods of time at virtually no cost in terms of forgone returns," he said.

Unlike other firms, where individuals are assigned responsibility for portfolios, at Tweedy, Browne three of the managing directors manage all of the firm's portfolios jointly.

"We use our own computer facilities to track all the portfolio positions and systematically allocate securities in an effort to minimize the amount of time spent on administration," he said. "The idea is to allow us to concentrate on research and analysis of investment opportunities rather than administrative portfolio details."

The investment process begins with significant amounts of screening to come up with lists of companies that initially fit the firm's investment qualifications. Once the firm finds a company that meets its expectations, an analyst tries to find out as much about the company as possible and then places the company on a Rolodex card. The difference between the cards that

Browne used in the early 1970s and the ones the firm uses today is that today's cards consist of more detailed reports than one or two equations.

"There is really a lot of grunt work that goes into researching a stock," said Browne. "Once we get the Rolodex card, all the managing directors review the information and work with analysts until we get to a level of comfort where we want to purchase the stock.

"Everything is put under the same microscope, whether it is domestic or international," he continued. "It really depends upon the company, and it basically comes down to us voting yea or nay on making the company part of the portfolio."

On average, the firm runs the Global Value Fund with about 190 names and the American Value Fund with 100 names. The funds hold $3.8 billion and $930 million, respectively.

Browne believes that what has helped make the firm so successful is its culture and the fact that none of its principals has ever left to join another investment company.

Throughout the firm's history, there have been only 11 principals. Five are currently active in the money management process on a day-to-day basis. Of the six former principals, three are still living and continue to have a significant portion of their assets managed by the firm. When we met, firm employees and their families had over $400 million invested with Tweedy, Browne through various accounts and its mutual funds.

"We function on the basis of a consensus, rather than as individual portfolio managers," Browne said. "This team approach and our focus on developing our corporate culture have provided us with a unique level of success over the last 80 years that I believe is unprecedented anywhere else on Wall Street."

What I Think . . .

When you talk about old-school money management firms, names like Goldman, Morgan, and Salomon come to mind. Very few people think of Tweedy, Browne, yet for more than 50 years the firm has been managing money. It has established quite an impressive track record, and yet it remains relatively unknown to the investing public.

Chris Browne likes it that way. He knows, as most of Wall Street does, that what his house does it does very well. He also knows that operating in relative obscurity is a good thing. Browne and his team have mastered the art of finding opportunities in markets outside the United States. While both Tweedy, Browne and Bernie Horn (who you will read about in the next chapter) may look at the same markets, their strategies are all their own, and both make sense.

Over the years, Browne and his colleagues have figured out what I believe is the best way to find opportunities in the market, and investors most likely will continue to benefit from the firm's methodology.

★ *chapter three* ★

SECTOR FUND MANAGERS

While the previous chapter profiled managers who focus on the broad market and look for investment opportunities across many different areas, this chapter deals with managers who focus on specific sectors of the market.

Unlike broad market investing, where the manager has to become a generalist who looks at various businesses in many areas, sector managers look only at companies in and around one section of the market. Some believe that this limits the opportunity for investment returns, while others believe it is the only way to know enough to make significant returns.

Most financial planners, stockbrokers, and investment professionals agree that the best way to construct a balanced portfolio is to invest in many areas of the market. This spreads the risk around so all the eggs are not in one basket. Sector funds provide the investor with an opportunity to build a portfolio of investments across multiple disciplines. By using them, an investor can get access to the best and brightest minds in specific areas without worrying that the fund managers know everything about a lot of things and nothing about specific things.

Over the past 5 to 10 years, sector investing has become quite popular. It has become so popular that many mutual fund companies have developed fund complexes that focus on specific industries or sectors of the market. For example, some fund companies now offer aggressive, moderate, and conservative funds, rather than just growth and value funds, for broad market investment but also for major sectors like health care and technology as well as a broad spectrum of other sector funds.

Marketers believe that the more product offerings the better so that should one sector turn bad, investors will roll their assets into another fund—say, from technology to financial services—or if one area of the technology sector is bad they can go into another, rather than withdrawing their money from the complex altogether.

Morningstar, Inc., which many consider to be the most thorough provider of data on the mutual fund industry, said that as of February 2002 there were over 1,060 sector funds, up from 180 in 1992. Some focus on a specific industry, like insurance or banking, rather than a broader segment of the market, like financial services. Within the specific areas, some fund complexes offer varying degrees of risk. For example, a fund company could have an aggressive technology fund, a conservative technology fund, and a technology fund that is both conservative and aggressive.

Still, the real problem for sector funds is that when the sector goes down, the fund usually goes down, too. There is little a fund complex can do besides offering other funds to pick up the assets.

"It makes no difference how well known or popular the manager or fund complex is," said Ellen McKay, a principal at the Optima Group Inc., a leading mutual fund marketing and communications firm in Connecticut. "When you run a sector fund you sort of live or die by the strength or weakness of the sector regardless of how the overall market is doing. Firms that offer one fund focused on one sector have a real problem. When the sector is hot, their fund is hot and the assets flow in, but when the sector gets into trouble, not only do the assets leave the fund because of poor performance, they have no other place to go within the organization."

One example of this is the Jacob Internet Fund, started in late 1999 by well-known mutual fund manager Ryan Jacob. The fund had a stellar first year, judged both by portfolio performance and by the ability to raise assets from investors. However, in light of the downturn in the market, the fund not only had terrible performance but lost most of its assets.

A little background: Jacob earned his stripes in 1998 when he took over the Kinetics Internet Fund, sold all its stocks except pure Internet companies, and rode the market to a staggering return of 196 percent. The fund had been up 12 percent in 1997. He then set up his own shop and began to manage his own fund.

Once the technology bubble burst and Internet stocks began to drop, the fund went into a free fall. The fund, originally offered at a share price of $10, had a net asset value of 93 cents as of February 1, 2002. The fund was dead last of all technology mutual funds at the end of 2000, having lost 79 percent of its value, and it was down an additional 60 percent by the end of August 2001. At its height in early 2000, the fund managed just over $300 million for investors; by August 2001 it managed just $30 million. The problem was not that the manager made bad decisions (one has to believe that all the stocks that Jacob and his team purchased were ones in which they believed). The problem was that the market decided that technology was over and that the stocks that everyone had thought could do nothing but go up had completely fallen out of favor. In fact, they fell to lows that no one ever thought they would see.

Regardless, Jacob still believes in the Internet and technology and continues to look for opportunities in the sector. He says that his biggest mistake was assuming that the Internet content companies could monetize their audiences as effectively as they thought they would. The fund, which was down over 30 percent in the first quarter of 2001, was still sticking to its guns.

"I lost a fortune with this fund," said one investor who requested anonymity. "It really turned out to be a terrible investment. I don't think it was Jacob's fault, however. I think it was the wrong investment at the wrong time. He had a previous record of success at his other fund, but timing just was not right."

Others, however, believe that Jacob is the poster boy for not letting past results predict future performance.

Wall Street is about timing; it is about constructing the right portfolio that will hold up under both good market conditions and bad market conditions. It is about constructing a portfolio of investments that complement each other but also react differently should the market move in one direction or another. The idea is to have a portfolio that allows you to truly diversify your holdings without taking out all of the upside. Most money management people suggest that any one sector should not make up more than 30 percent of an investor's portfolio.

Some people, on the other hand, diversify so much that they aren't able to make a significant return on their investments. The key is to get the right mix to ensure that you have the opportunity to be successful when the market or the sector turns.

Over time your sectors will get hot. The problem is that nobody knows when any sector will become better than any other sector. That's why you need to be diversified and willing to ride out the market's ups and downs.

Samuel Isaly

When it comes to active health care mutual fund managers, there are not many who have been in the industry as long as Sam Isaly.

Isaly, who started his career at Chase Manhattan Bank as drug industry analyst in 1966, is the manager of the Eaton Vance World Health Sciences fund. He took the fund over from "a bunch of doctors" in 1989, when it had just $2.5 million in assets in one mutual fund. In the summer of 2001, his money management company was probably the tenth-largest health care fund organization in the United States. It included the original mutual fund with over $1.4 billion, a group of hedge funds with over $800 million, a private equity fund with $200 million, and a group of offshore accounts that have more than $600 million in assets under management.

He got into fund management as an outgrowth of his research business. Initially Isaly's company would complete research on the sector and sell its investment ideas to firms, including Fidelity Investments and T. Rowe Price. Once the firms decided that Isaly's organization, more specifically its mutual fund, was a competitor, they decided not to purchase information from "the competition" any longer.

"We were in the research business and still are today, but at the time we sold our ideas to other money management firms. Initially we used the fund as a showcase for our best research ideas, and then we would sell our research to institutions based on how the fund performed," he said. "Interestingly, the tail started to wag the dog. As the fund began to perform well, many of the firms we were selling research to no longer wanted to purchase it from us. So now all of our ideas go into our own products."

Isaly's company, OrbiMed Advisors LLC, consists of investment professionals who come from both a business background and a science background. They focus solely on the health care and biotechnology sectors, which he says tend to operate with tunnel vision.

He decided to go out on his own because he was "never successful" in a bureaucracy.

"I failed in at least two bureaucracies, maybe three, and I don't mean I did bad work. What I mean by failure is that I did not become the president or chairman and had no prospect of ever doing so," he said. "I realized that I don't have the skills to thrive in a bureaucracy and am much better in places where an entrepreneurial and independent spirit is needed."

While initially Isaly was not quite happy about being a drug industry analyst, he said that it proved to be exactly what he needed in order to get to where he is today. He believes that had he been assigned to another sector he might not have been as successful.

"This sector has been and will be a great sector to work in, because it has historically gone up. So a drug analyst is always responsible for stocks that win, so the drug analysts always get promoted," he said. "If you survey chief investment analysts from firms around the country, I bet you will find that a considerable amount of them started out as drug analysts. It is not that they are smarter than everyone else; they just happened to be in the right sector. If they were steel analysts during the same period, I bet they are still steel analysts today because the stocks never went up and they were not promoted through the organization. I did not get stuck being a drug analyst; I got anointed by it and blessed with it, because I might still be a steel analyst."

Today the OrbiMed team, which consists of analysts, traders, and office professionals, covers approximately 500 public companies around the globe. Compared to other sectors like technology or financial services, it operates in a relatively small universe of possible investment opportunities. Still, over the past few years, that universe has grown quite rapidly. Both new and old-line health care and biotechnology companies have been making considerable advances in understanding genes and developing drugs and medical devices.

"The companies we look at represent about 10 percent of the worldwide stock market," he said. "Technology makes up about 20 percent of the worldwide stock market, and financial services represent about 15 percent, meaning that nearly half the worldwide market is concentrated in three sectors. We are happy to stick with our 10 percent and do it right."

Isaly's first step in managing money is to find good companies that meet his broad investment criteria. The second step is to reduce those companies to a list that is worthy of being in the portfolio.

"Usually one in ten of our ideas ends up in the portfolio," he said. "We like to keep the fund concentrated, which allows us to follow the companies closely, talk to management, and really stay on top of them."

When it comes to the investment process, Isaly and his team try to stay focused and try to avoid spending their time on "bad things." Each of the investment professionals covers approximately 300 companies to decide if they are worthy of being in the portfolio.

Everybody on the team has a group of companies within the sector that they follow. Isaly's specialty is the large U.S.-based and European health care companies. When we met in the summer of 2001, the fund had positions in two of his companies: Novartis AG and Monsanto Company.

"Regardless of the company, we seem to be a welcome investor," he said, "because we are long-term holders and are probably perceived to bring some level of credibility to a company when the public learns that we have invested in the stock."

Isaly and his team are in constant contact with the companies that are in the portfolio. While he knows that some people think of him as "a pain" and "crusty," for the most part the managers are interested in talking to him about their companies.

"I am sure some people don't like to hear from us, but the proper response to our inquiries is, we own them and therefore they are working for us, and we would hope that they listen to us," he said. "In each case it is different, and depending on the company, it depends on how strong a position we are in. If we own 10 percent of the company, management is more willing to talk to us than when we own 4 percent of the stock."

In general the mutual fund portfolio consists of approximately 40 positions, ranging in size from less than 1 percent to over 10 percent of the assets under management. Regardless of the size of the position, some member of OrbiMed is talking to the company's management team.

"Everybody has a bunch of bananas," he said. "They find the best, and they surface the ideas at a meeting. They have to make a case as to why we should make room for something in the portfolio. In order to get something in, something has to come out.

"We usually push something out when something better comes along," he continued. "The hard part is trying to figure out what to sell. And we very much try to resist name count expansion, so it is pretty much one in, one out."

Yet as assets have grown, Isaly has expanded the number of names in the portfolio. In the summer of 2001, the main portfolio—the Eaton Vance World Health Services fund—included 42 names.

Unlike other health care and biotech managers who worry about slippage (the ability to move in and out of a stock freely without the price changing during the trade), Isaly believes his fund can grow not by adding more companies but by increasing the fund's stake in a particular stock.

"We have adopted the policy that rather than own more names, we own higher percentages of the companies in which we invest," he said. "The down side to this policy is that if we make a mistake, there is no way out and we will become permanent investors."

Isaly said that he is willing to become a permanent investor if need be, to pursue his strategy of finding great companies and sticking with them. "If we believe in the company, we are willing to be investors for as long as it takes," he said.

OrbiMed breaks the sector into pieces, the better to focus on specifics: big pharmaceutical companies, biotechnology stocks, small-cap and large-cap stocks, discovery and distribution stocks, and high-risk and low-risk stocks.

"All of the areas are equal to each other and carry as much weight as the others in the overall portfolio," he said.

Isaly evaluates a company by looking at its people and

management, its technology, its financial strength, and the timeliness of its products.

"We need to be able to foresee a change in the company's stock price based on our research. If we can't see it, we won't get into it," he said. "Recently, we started a buying program on a company that we don't believe will make any significant move for about three years, but we want to be there when it happens, so we started it now. By the time we are done buying, we will own 4 percent of the company, and we will wait."

When we met in the summer of 2001, the fund included a mixture of stocks with various levels of risk, opportunity, and expected growth rates. Isaly's team put them together to create a portfolio that offered considerable promise. During the first half of 2001, the fund had a minimal amount of turnover and had stopped buying new stocks.

"This has been a particularly slow period for us. While we like to hold onto things for a long period of time, on average about three years, we also like to find new things and make them part of the portfolio," he said.

The Eaton Vance World Health Sciences fund has a record that goes back to 1989, back to when there was no biotechnology sector in which to invest.

"When we started, there were two dozen pharmaceutical companies around the world that you could invest in," he said. "Since then, however, a whole lot of companies have emerged, and we have kept up with that by creating our ability to assess the new skills at the same time the new skills have arrived.

"Now I have an MIT Ph.D. here because he is good at understanding the new technology and skills that are coming down the pike," he continued.

Isaly believes the health and biotechnology sector will continue to thrive for many years, because the pace of change is so dramatic.

"Drugs will continue to get more specific and less toxic," he said. "We believe that the continued advances will be numerically demonstrated in the number of new drugs that are approved for use in the United States."

Right now each year approximately 45 new drugs are approved for use, and Isaly believes that number will double over the next 10 years. He believes that, while technology was the sector for the past decade, biotechnology is the place to be for this decade, because the pace of change has begun to accelerate.

"The amount of new drugs that get approved is a measure of productivity as well as providing the opportunity for companies to address diseases that are currently not addressed by the industry," he said. "I propose that the world's best-selling drug will be a drug for Alzheimer's. While I don't know who will make it or what it will consist of, it is [a drug for] that sort of problem, aging mental degeneration, that will find widespread use and outsell any of the drugs on the market.

"This decade belongs to me," he added. "I plan on continuing to be managing money in this sector at least until the end of the decade or I get hit by a bus."

When potential investors question him about his and his firm's ability to pick stocks or the strength of his strategy, Isaly refers them to something he calls "the Burt letter," a trophy of sorts that hangs on the wall in his office in midtown Manhattan.

The letter, from one of Wall Street's most famous authors and a champion of indexing, asks for Isaly's opinion of a company called Gene Logic, a Maryland-based genomic company. Burton Malkiel, the author of *A Random Walk Down Wall Street*, wrote the letter.[1] The book, which most will agree is a must-read, says that investors are much better buying index funds than individual stocks, because no stock picker can beat the law of averages over long periods of time.

"It is quite an accomplishment," said Isaly. "Here is a champion of indexing asking for my opinion on a particular stock. That must say something about how good we are, or at least that we know what we are doing."

★ ★ ★

What I Think . . .

It's probably safe to say that Isaly is one of the most respected biotechnology and health care money managers in the business. He has also been at it longer than most. Isaly climbed through the ranks of Wall Street and landed squarely on top. He is a force to be reckoned with, and people respect him for it. And while some may think his funds are too big and that the opportunities are not very clear, with Isaly it seems that these things just don't matter.

His investment style at OrbiMed really sets him apart from others focusing on this sector. His team eats, drinks, and sleeps biotech, and its efforts have paid off. The events surrounding "the Burt letter" pretty much say it all. I don't think people need anything more to understand why they should invest with him.

Bernie Horn

Bernie Horn became interested in Wall Street when he was washing windows at Boston's Logan Airport. His uncle had gotten him the summer job, and during his breaks he would read the weekly financial newspaper *Barron's*, because he found it lying around the terminals.

"The job at the airport taught me two things. First, it taught me about Wall Street and the markets, but, more important, it taught me the value of a good education," he said.

Horn, who is the principal and fund manager of Boston-based Polaris Capital Management Inc., said his interest in working on the Street also came from his father, who was a good bargain hunter.

"My father taught me the importance of getting a good feel for the market, whether it be the real estate market or the stock market," he said. "Once he got an understanding of the market, it was easy for him to pick off a really good value. A lot of my bargain-hunting expertise came from the experience of watching him buy things."

Horn went to Boston's Northeastern University as a cooperative education student. The five-year co-op program has students alternate semesters between working and taking classes. His co-op job was in the finance department of the Gillette Company.

"At Northeastern, I got a really good dose of accounting and finance, and began to understand how the numbers in the annual report and the 10-K got there," he said. "When I first arrived at Gillette, it was very much a sales organization, but over time it changed into a company that focused on finance and profitability."

He continued, "My classroom experience at Northeastern and real-life experience at Gillette gave me great exposure to the overall business of finance and the role it plays in a company."

While Horn was in school, a guest speaker in the finance

class talked about options, and that gave him a whole new view of the markets.

At the time, all options were traded over the counter; there were no exchange-traded options. Horn persuaded one of his professors to let him do an independent study of options. He came across articles written by Fischer Black, Robert Merton, and Paul Samuelson, who were working just across the river at the Massachusetts Institute of Technology.

Horn crossed over to MIT and met with the fathers of option-pricing models and ended up going to its Sloan School of Business for an MBA.

"Going to business school [after Northeastern] was an unusual thing to do, because I had the work experience, and most people graduated and took a job at their co-op company. Because I had overdosed on finance theory, I thought going to business school was the best thing for me because it let me continue to learn about finance and money management," he said.

Horn entered MIT in 1978, graduating in 1980. At Sloan, he was able to avoid many of the basic courses because of prior course work and spent most of his time focusing on accelerated finance classes.

"It was a very unique time to be studying options," he said. "I was able to work with Fischer Black and Bob Merton to do my thesis on pricing models."

During the summer between his first and second year of business school, Horn went to work in the institutional options department at Donaldson, Lufkin & Jenrette for Matthew "Mike" Gladstein. Gladstein had been working with Merton and Scholes on a paper that detailed what they called the 90/10 money management strategy (90 percent invested in Treasury bills, 10 percent in calls). He gave Horn the chance not only to study the theories but to practice them as well.

"It was that summer working on Wall Street that really convinced me that I wanted to be in this business," he said. "I was just so excited that I could not wait to get into it, nor could I wait and spend three or four years as an analyst covering some industry and have them decide if they were going to let me manage money someday."

Horn entered his second year at Sloan intent on becoming a money manager. He focused on learning how to be an entrepreneur and working on a business plan for a money management firm that was based on the 90/10 strategy.

"During the summer, my job was to work with one of the first Apple 2 computers that came off the assembly line. I programmed randomly generated stock prices and the option values on those stocks into it," he said. "The program would simulate how to write covered calls on an equity, providing a strategy that would moderate the overall risk of the portfolio."

When Horn and his bosses explained what they were doing to managers of institutional portfolios, they found that many did not understand what they were talking about.

"Making these presentations and seeing the way these people reacted convinced me without a doubt that I could survive in this business," he said.

The 90/10 strategy consists of putting 90 percent of the assets into Treasury bills at a double-digit interest rate—at the time inflation was high, and Treasuries were yielding in the double digits—and putting the remaining 10 percent into diversified call options.

"The idea was that if the market totally crashed and everything went to zero, you would still have all of your money because of the fixed-income investment. If the market took off, the portfolio of calls would carry you through," he said. "It was effectively a way to change the shape of the portfolio's return distribution. It was a very well-diversified portfolio that was a prudent strategy for risk-averse investors."

Horn's business plan called for him to market the strategy to pension funds and others he felt would be interested.

"We did every form of networking and marketing to tell people about the strategy and get them interested in investing with us," he said. "What we found, however, was that most of the institutions we went to had prohibitions against owning options. People thought that option trading took place in a Wild West type of market and really did not know enough about options to understand how or why the strategy would work. And at the time they were unwilling to learn."

To keep the cash flow going while he was working on building his money management business, Horn did some consulting for a firm in Boston that was developing an international stock mutual fund. Through this, he became interested in learning about the exceptions to the market efficiencies that Fischer Black had been writing about at MIT. Horn started to look at one area in particular, something that Black called the value strategy: buying low price-to-earnings ratio stocks. He realized that the strategy fit his personality—the one he inherited from his father—of bargain hunting, and decided to focus on it.

"Modern portfolio theory would say that the optimal combination of risky assets was to buy a well-diversified portfolio, which was defined as buying things in proportion to their market cap," he said.

Horn believes that when he came into the business, things were completely different from how they are today. Then he was doing something unique because, unlike other people, he had experience with something called the personal computer.

"My experience with technology made me realize that I did not need to have a team of analysts running around covering every single company. I could use the computer to screen data, and from there cover the companies directly," he said. "I felt very strongly then, and still do 21 years later, that the best combination of risky assets is a portfolio of global companies, because it gives the optimal amount of diversification."

Because he was not working with a firm that was married to a domestic-only strategy, Horn was able to develop a fresh philosophy of building a business and managing assets based on a global strategy.

"Value was time-tested when I started, and I decided to focus on global because there were very few competitors in the market when I was starting out in 1981," he said. "I felt that many of the existing money managers were at a significant disadvantage because they were limiting themselves to domestic companies."

Horn spent lots of time building a retail and institutional money management business but also continued to act as a consultant. He helped organizations, including the Ford Foundation and State Street Bank, to build international money management programs.

"I could see that there was a lot of interest in this area. I learned from my consultants that the key to success would be to establish a five-year track record," he said. "I felt that if I started in 1980, by 1985 the world would clearly understand the importance of a global strategy and they would flock to my product."

Unfortunately for Horn, investors didn't buy into his idea so readily. Still, over the past 20 years, people have started to shift their investments globally, and he believes that now that he has a long track record, assets will begin to flow into his firm.

"There are not many competitors that have as long and as strong a track record managing global equities as we do," he said, "using the same discipline and philosophy over this long a period of time."

When we met in the fall of 2001, Horn was managing just under $125 million in both a no-load mutual fund and a series of separate accounts.

He has structured his organization around the idea that he manages the firm's assets himself. Analysts help him with research, but he makes all the decisions.

"I believe that people should make a decision on where they are going to invest their money based on the person managing the portfolio and not the strength of the institution," he said. "If I were to be hit by a bus, investors would need to reevaluate their investment because I would no longer be managing the portfolio. It is no different than when Peter Lynch left Magellan. People needed to make a decision as to whether they believed in the new manager."

Horn believes that the key to his success has been that his investors know who is managing their money and whether he is capable of making investment decisions.

"I have built a business around the idea of making it very clear to clients that they know who is managing their money—someone with a lot of experience. If that person is no longer here, then they should reevaluate the organization," he said.

"I think people need to take an active role in managing their money. Unfortunately, the market is such that people don't really seem to care," he continued. "People are more interested in buying into the brand of the organization rather than the specific manager."

One of the things that Horn believes has helped his performance is that he has been following many companies in his portfolio for more than a decade.

"I understand the companies in my portfolio. I don't rely on an analyst or nonproprietary research to provide me with information," he said. "I do the work myself, and that is who I am asking people to entrust their money to."

Horn uses a three-step process to uncover opportunities. He begins with a global valuation model to determine which countries and which industries are overvalued or undervalued by ranking them.

"I use aggregate company data like price to book and price to cash flow and interest-rate information to help me identify things that may look attractive," he said.

The second step is look at stocks at a company level to affirm that the things that look quite attractive actually are.

"The point of the first two steps of the process is quite simple," he said. "I don't want to cover 20,000 companies in my database. I only want to look at companies that are undervalued. I want to see that if I buy them at the current price, I am going to earn [a higher] excess return than if I were to buy an index fund.

"People are not paying me to get them an average return on the stock market, which is what they could get if they bought an index fund," he continued. "They are paying to perform better than the index."

Horn has designed his stock-selection process to generate returns in excess of 200 basis points above his benchmark index. He believes that if he continues to generate returns of that level he will always be in the top quartile of funds with a similar investment strategy.

"I only look at companies that I can discount the present

value of future cash flows at 8 percent over inflation," he said. "I want to avoid companies that do not fit into this model because those types of companies are going to destroy value for my clients and myself."

Horn then focuses his research on the companies that fit into this universe of investment ideas. He screens for ideas with some regularity, but for the most part he finds the kinds of inefficiencies he is looking for in annual reports and regulatory filings.

"People expect that the markets are highly efficient and that everything is fairly priced according to the amount of information that is available to these companies," he said. "But, if that was the case, then how does one explain the dot-com bubble or the Nasdaq bubble? It is because humans take the most recent past and, through bad statistics, project that most recent past into the future indefinitely.

"That simple human behavior creates opportunities for me," he continued. "What I am looking for are the inefficiencies in the market that create these undervalued or overvalued opportunities."

Horn does not look for inefficiencies that would predict that Coca-Cola's stock, while it may be correctly priced relative to the estimates, may not be correct when the market closes and the company releases its earnings.

"In my universe, things do not change so rapidly," he said. "I can look at the data daily to see if things have changed and something has become a good value and it should become part of the portfolio."

Using a discount rate of 8 percent is background for Horn when he looks at the domestic market, because the interest rate is much the same for everyone in that segment. When he looks at companies abroad, though, he pays particular attention to interest rates because the cost of capital can be significant.

"I incorporate real yields, because in a very elegant way it solves the problem of exchange rate risk," he said. "If I am looking for 8 percent and it turns out that the sovereign debt in a country is yielding 8 percent, why should I invest in the riskier equity stream when I can get the same return in real terms as the sovereign debt?"

Horn will not necessarily buy the debt but instead will incorporate the interest rate information into his equation for looking at stocks in that country.

"I am not going to buy an equity that is going to pay me the same return as a debt instrument," he said. "I am going to want to pay much less for the equity stream because the debt return implies that there is a devaluation coming, and I need to take that into account when looking at the exchange rate problem."

His universe of opportunities gets even smaller when he screens the list for discount rates by country.

"With the Fed cutting 400 basis points off of the short end of the curve in a very short period of time and then seeing how the rest of the world reacts to the cuts, you can imagine that my discount rates and what I am doing are shifting around a bit," he said.

By using a significant amount of investment technology and a stream of data from around the world, Horn can screen all the companies in his universe in 24 to 36 hours.

"Technology provides me with a significant amount of time to leverage. Instead of looking at 20,000 companies, I can look at 300 or 400," he said. "By using proprietary technology that has been built over the last 20 years, I am able to spend my time working smarter rather than harder."

Once Horn comes up with his potential investments, he switches to fundamental analysis, scrubbing down the financial statement "real hard" to make sure the database wasn't fooling him.

"I look much closer at the financial statements to really understand the company," he said. "I want to know if there is any hidden dilution or if the cash flows are being pumped by the liquidation of working capital because the company is having a difficult sales environment."

Horn believes that his task has become very manageable over the years and that the database does most of the difficult work up front.

"Once I establish my universe, I am able to focus on specific aspects of the company and determine rather quickly if it is really an attractive investment," he said. "If they still look really attractive, then I can get into the detective work and make a decision if the investing in the company makes sense."

Horn likes to use classic Graham-and-Dodd-style analysis to evaluate companies. He also likes to meet with managers around the globe. And while in the early 1980s he often had trouble with communicating, his language skills have improved and more and more companies are doing business in English, so things are a bit easier than before.

"If you talk to a couple of hundred management teams a year for 20 years, you eventually pick up some pretty good skills at interviewing and detective work," he said.

He believes that he can tell a lot about a company by talking not only to the management teams but also to customers, suppliers, and competitors.

Horn sees his strategy as borderless. Because he is looking all over the world, he feels that he cannot mimic an index. Typically the areas that make up an index tend to be the best performers over the past few years; he is looking for opportunities that will become the best performers over the next few years.

"Global is all about working with both sides of your brain. You just need to constantly be questioning everything," he said. "And if you don't, you are probably going to be blindsided. It is all about getting that slightly better information advantage, and the only way you are going to get it is by looking at everything."

While Horn travels extensively to find opportunities, he uses what he calls a measured, disciplined, and deliberate approach to doing so.

"There has to be a reason for me to get on a plane and make a trip," he said. "I am not interested in running around the world to chase ideas. I go when I find something that is undervalued and try to spend my time very deliberately.

"It is a full-time intellectual challenge," he continued. "As we used to say at MIT, it's like taking a drink out of a fire hydrant."

★ ★ ★

What I Think . . .

Bernie Horn is the type of investment pro who never quite gets the recognition that he deserves. Horn has been practicing his craft for more than 20 years and has built a very successful small business. Still, investors need to do some work to find his funds and, because most investors are lazy, they won't.

His approach to finding opportunities abroad is quite remarkable. Although his success could have been expected (I mean, how many people really decide that they want to work on Wall Street while they are sweeping floors?), the odds against it were pretty great and yet he achieved his goal. Now it seems that Horn is focusing on growing his business, and he'll probably reach that goal as well.

Gerry Malone and Peter Anastos

In the comics, we have the Dynamic Duo. Batman leads and Robin follows, providing backup and help to his trusted friend and adviser. One thing that we all know for sure is that when you are fighting supervillains, two good guys are better than one.

Can the same be said for managing money? While many believe that egos and personalities get in the way of making good investment decisions, over the past 10 years a Wall Street dynamic duo of sorts has been making it work. Not only have they built a successful franchise at one of the leading mutual fund complexes, but also they have remained friends while doing so and seem to be quite happy. The difference between them and the Batman and Robin duo is that each of them is Batman and they have 17 or so Robins.

The partnership began just over 10 years ago when Peter Anastos was asked to manage Alliance Capital Management's technology fund. He was told to find a co-manager and someone who could continue to work on developing the firm's technology research department.

"I had known Gerry for quite some time—we had traveled the same circuit, covering technology—and we invited him over to Alliance to interview for the job," said Anastos. "He really fit in here, because he had a number of the qualities the firm and [that] the co-manager needed to have in order to be successful—ambition and conviction."

"I was offered the job in early 1992 and came to the firm at the end of the first quarter, and Peter and I were the entire technology department at Alliance," Malone said. "We decided early on to carve the technology world up between us in terms of research coverage, and we continue to do so as we manage the portfolio [today]."

Many believe that comanagement of a fund is a recipe for either great success or complete disaster. This dynamic duo has been able to achieve the former.

"You have to respect, trust, and like your partner, and if you do you are going to be a team and work together for the benefit of your mutual and shared success. If those things don't apply, sooner or later it is going to break down," said Anastos. "It is like a marriage."

When the two came on board, the fund was a small piece of the Alliance pie, with just over $140 million in assets. A dedicated portfolio manager ran it, but there was really no consistency in management from year to year.

"The managers would come in, have a good year, and leave without any loyalty to Alliance, so the firm decided to get an analyst involved because the culture, as an aside, is to have strong research. The thinking was if an analyst was involved there would be consistency and loyalty, and the business would grow," said Anastos.

So how do two analysts who had met a few times at industry conferences and on the golf course build a successful business?

The first thing is to check your ego at the door, and the second is to realize that the market you are covering is too big for one person. By splitting it up into pieces, you are much more likely to find good ideas than if you did it all yourself.

"The firm was not interested in having one of us be a senior manager or anything like that. They really wanted us to operate equally, so the key was to find personalities that fit and ensure that there are no hidden agendas and to focus on mutual success," said Anastos. "What made sense was that both of us had had success in different areas of technology, so we sort of cut the technology universe with a butter knife to avoid any sharp edges, so that by design we would have some overlap. That gives us things to talk about and forces us to communicate about ideas so that you don't become xenophobic."

"The nice thing about technology is that sector is sort of like a food chain so the information takes you from one area to another and really gives you perspective about the whole thing," said Malone. "That has kept the working relationship focused on finding the impact of the information on the total portfolio."

Take, for example, their decision to invest in the semiconductor industry. Anastos is the semiconductor analyst, while Malone covers the personal computer (PC) market.

"I would tell him that I really like Intel and tell him what is happening in the market from [the semiconductor maker's] perspective, and he would say, 'Well, that is interesting. Let me tell you what is going on from the personal computer market side,'" said Anastos. "So we have this dovetail—overlap if you will—of information on trends. He would buy Dell [Computer Corporation] for the portfolio and I would buy Intel, and we would structure the portfolio accordingly."

The idea of team management is very important to both Anastos and Malone. They don't split assets; they simply build what they believe is the most diversified portfolio possible.

Splitting assets is “not the way we think; it just would not work for us,” said Anastos.

Instead they work from their convictions and construct the portfolio based on their ideas of the market. Neither has veto power over the other, and they don’t have to agree—indeed, sometimes they don’t!

“If Peter feels that the portfolio should head in a certain way and I don’t necessarily agree, we will go there and construct the portfolio accordingly. What we will do is follow a consistent style,” said Malone. “We have always run a portfolio construction process focused on diversification. Therefore we will never let one industry be more than 25 percent of the portfolio, and we will never let one stock be more than 5 percent. By setting limits like that, by definition we are meeting our goal of running a diversified technology portfolio.”

Both Malone and Anastos believe that this is truly the only way to run a technology fund. It allows them to create a diversified portfolio with exposure to all areas, instead of having large concentrations in a few areas.

“Some of our competitors do not do this, and they will run a portfolio with 50 percent of the fund’s assets in semis or something like that,” said Malone. “Our research has been broad enough to tell us that there have been a lot of subsectors, and the portfolio construction says don’t put all your eggs in one basket.”

Managing a technology fund regardless of market conditions is very difficult, but this team has managed to be successful by sticking with what they know.

“In the beginning, we sort of looked at the industry and said, ‘I am going to do semis because I have done it, and you are going to do PC because you have done it,’ and basically we have stuck to the initial approach," said Anastos. "And as the technology sector has evolved, so has our coverage."

Currently the two focus solely on managing the portfolio and work with a team of analysts to develop ideas for the fund. At the time we met, there were nine analysts working on the fund in the United States and eight based in London and Asia.

"The infrastructure of the operation has changed as the technology sector has expanded," said Anastos. "The only thing that has remained constant is that Gerry and I have remained co–portfolio managers."

Since they began managing the fund it has performed very well, both for investors and as a business for Alliance. The first significant event came about a month or two after they took over—when the market turned and they saw the assets drop to $125 million. While they have passed many milestones since then, the most memorable was when they reached $15 billion in assets at the height of the technology craze. At the time we met in the summer of 2001, the fund held just under $8 billion and comprised 48 stocks.

"When you are at $140 million in assets, the fund really does not generate much in fees to the firm, but when you reach $15 billion, it becomes a serious business and everything changes," said Malone. "It represents significant income to the firm and becomes something people stand up and take notice of."

Their fund carries a 1 percent management fee that goes directly to the adviser, which means that it was generating approximately $80 million in revenue to the company when we met as its assets were just under $8 billion.

So how do you go from managing $140 million to $15 billion? Besides being in the right place at the right time, you need the right infrastructure to handle the growth.

"When they write the history of technology, the 1990s were *it*. It was when everything worked: Technology asserted itself, productivity paid off, consumers embraced technology, and companies said, 'Technology is my infrastructure,'" said Malone. "Spending went wild, and everything seemed to be working, and people wanted to take part in it, so for us our fund was positioned perfectly to take part in the ride."

Alliance had positioned itself as a firm that had a reputation for research-driven quality products and had a strategy that fit the technology boom. Over the years the firm had had some pretty good numbers, technology as a whole was beating the S&P and the other indexes, and people were looking for a place to invest. So the duo launched the Peter and Gerry show.

"We went on the road and told our story. It was, 'We are the analysts that know this stuff, we are part of a firm that has the resources to take advantage of this opportunity, and you as investors should have a special place in your portfolio for tech,'" said Malone. "The planets really aligned for us, and of course everything culminated with the whole Internet boom and bust."

And while it may seem easy to some, both believe that running the fund will continue to be hard work, whether the fund's assets soar to $30 billion or sink to $125 million.

"For me it has been hard since day one. While Alliance is a great firm, first of all, it does not suffer fools lightly, and secondly, I don't like to be wrong because it is embarrassing when your NAV [net asset value] is published in the newspaper every day," said Anastos. "You are in a goldfish bowl here, but for me it has been stressful all along. Because the difference between a hundred million and a billion is a zero, the real change was that suddenly you are running money; shareholders are depending on you; you've got an NAV published in the paper, which reflects on us and the firm; and it is stressful, regardless of size."

One thing that has remained constant throughout the growth of the fund has been the fund's mission statement that the two drafted when they took over.

"We wanted something that would work. We said that we wanted to focus on quality companies, companies that are changing the world that we can own for a long time. That turned out to be the appropriate strategy for what then became this huge growth and demand for tech," said Malone. "So the fund was able to scale with the impact of these companies."

So when Cisco went from its initial public offering to a market capitalization of $500 billion, the managers did not have to change their strategy much, because the fund was growing with the industry.

"Some things have changed, but for the most part things are the same," said Malone. "We have always wanted to own around 50 names and always wanted to bet on the top 10, which have always been 30 percent to 35 percent of the portfolio and in turn added a significant amount of return to the portfolio.

"I remember the first time we owned more than a million shares of a stock. It was Oracle and it split, and I could not believe that we had so much," he continued. "Now almost every stock we own, we own a million shares of it."

Both believe that not only has the strength of the Alliance name and the firm's infrastructure helped in terms of building an investor base but it has also helped in providing access to information.

"Management wants Alliance to be a shareholder in their companies because, first, we are not a run-and-gun shop, and, second, we are big," said Anastos. "Companies look at us as partners in their business because they know that we are going to take a nice position in the stock and stick with them for a while—which creates access to not only the companies we are investing in but also their competitors and their suppliers."

Malone and Anastos believe that the technology sector is so Darwinian that they have to be very careful about taking a position. Saying that the stock is such a great story that you are going to invest in it for the next three or four years could be suicidal.

"We do not buy stock because there is going to be an analyst meeting and there is going to be a buzz around it or the company is going to get a contract or that there are going to be expectations by a penny which could cause the stock to go up 5 or 10 percent. We are not traders," said Anastos. "We also do not spend time focusing on timing the market or looking at things for the short term. Instead we look at things that have some staying power."

The managers' objective is to buy companies with great opportunities that warrant their becoming long-term positions. They do not buy them to sit on them for three years to see if it is going to work; they buy the stocks and keep them as long as the companies meet their expectations.

While they enjoy learning from the managers of the companies they own in the portfolio, they also realize that sometimes the picture the company executives paint is too rosy. That's especially true now that most companies compensate their management teams with stock options, which focuses them on keeping the stock price as high as possible.

The fund is driven solely by fundamental analysis. The pair does not use screens to weed out companies; instead they are essentially watching technology evolve.

"You can see things happen, see things change, see companies change their focus or their strategy and create new areas of interest, and we go to see them, meet them, and try to understand their strategy and decide if it makes sense or not," said Malone. "The great thing about tech is that something is always new. It isn't like we are at the bottom of the skill cycle."

Both men enjoy auto racing and believe that some of the skills they use to move quickly and safely around the track are analogous to managing the portfolio.

"I remember an instructor one day on the track telling me that when you are going into a turn you should really not focus on the road *there*. You need to be looking at the road way ahead of you," said Anastos. "Technology is very similar, because when you are driving a car at high rates of speed it's the same as the way we live our lives here. The rate of change in technology is very, very fast. It is the most dynamic industry and more and more people are short-term oriented. What that means to me is that they are looking at the road in front of the car, and I think the biggest money is made when you are looking ahead and are catching big change, not small change. Big impact, longer lasting; short-term change, shorter impact, shorter lasting, higher turnover."

Malone and Anastos believe that the best investment is a small company with a big idea. While it may take some time for it to affect the portfolio, sometimes it may represent several companies and thus offer new investment opportunities for the portfolio. For example, a small company may have a new type of technology. If it works others will follow it and an opportunity will be created. Initially, because it is a small company it will not have an effect on the return on the portfolio, but as it gets bigger and becomes an industry unto itself it will effect the significantly.

"We want to get into a stock as low as we can and still manage the risk, and get out as the returns are peaking or we see them peaking, because once they are peaking, if you don't get out you are going to be screwed," said Malone. "We are paid to know how things work and have a certain success factor."

While technology is changing daily and the stocks are moving rapidly, many things are not so new. Having 50-plus combined years of market experience doesn't hurt these two. Take, for example, the business-to-business software company explosion. Both had been following software companies for years, and they know that the business model is highly leveraged—that is, sales driven and based on what the product does. Just because it was business-to-business didn't mean it was totally different; it was just a different medium of delivery.

"All industries, without exception, consolidate down to a single winner or a small handful of winners. That consolidation takes place before the peak of the S curve in the industry," said Anastos. "Take Cisco, which we got into real early, but for a while we owned 3Com, Cabletron, and Bay Networks. At one time you could not say that Cisco was a better company, but little by little it started to break out. So what was maturity then was not maturity of the idea or the opportunity, but it was maturity of the opportunity for the wanna-bes and for the also-rans."

Anastos and Malone are now faced with a different challenge. Now that Cisco has won it all, the question becomes whether it is now maturing. Has its opportunity been fully exploited, and is it just the best of a lot of mediocrities?

"When a company is maturing, regardless of how good it is, it is time to get out," said Anastos. "The hard part is knowing when it is maturing."

What I Think . . .

Partnerships are hard work even in good times, so think how difficult they must be in bad times. Regardless of what the market is like or how their sector is doing, it seems that Malone and Anastos have found a formula that works.

When it comes to technology funds, there are few that have as long a track record as theirs. It was easy to start a fund and raise a whole lot of money in the mid-1990s, but what are those managers doing now? Some funds have been reduced to nothing, others to next to nothing, but Malone and Anastos continue to weather the storm, dodging the fallen trees in their path because they can see the entire forest. The evolution of their fund is quite a remarkable story, but it is a long story and one that makes them better managers and worthy of investment.

Chris Davis

If you ever see a man in a suit and tie riding a bicycle through the streets of New York, take another look, because it just might be Chris Davis of Davis Selected Advisors.

Davis, who started riding his bike to work about six years ago, says it is one of the greatest quality-of-life improvements he was able to make and keep up with.

"I don't have time to go to the gym every day, so now I get some exercise every day. It isn't that far, so I can ride in a suit and carry my briefcase," he said. "It is so great. It is much faster than riding the bus or taking the subway or walking, and it really makes life easier."

Most money managers have interesting stories about how they got into the business, but there are few who were destined for the industry from birth like Davis. He has the money management business running through his veins. Both his grandfather and father are Wall Street legends. There are great stories about how both built enormous fortunes by staying focused on their convictions and their investment principles.

Davis took a rather unusual route to the family business, though. First he earned a master's degree in philosophy, and then he went to the seminary to become a priest. He was in France working as a pastoral assistant at a church in Paris when he decided that the priesthood was not for him. He returned to Boston in the late 1980s and tried teaching, but then decided that he wanted to pursue the family business after all.

"I had spent a lot of summers working for my grandfather and my father, helping them with the research side of the business," he said. "And I decided that I would pursue a career in it like they had. However, I realized that while I knew a lot about researching businesses, I knew nothing about the number-crunching side and that in order to be successful I would need to learn."

Davis took a job in a State Street firm's training program and began taking courses at night in an effort to learn "all the things" he didn't study in college. After a while he took a job as an analyst working for a start-up money management shop in New York.

"It was from this point on that I knew that I wanted to become an analyst and specifically focus in the financial services area," he said. "It was right in the middle of the savings and loan debacle. Partly because of what I learned from my father and because of the fact that my grandfather was a specialist in the insurance industry, it always intrigued me that he made a fortune in it and that Buffett was making a fortune in financial services as well."

Davis believes that one of the reasons that his grandfather and others were so successful in investing in the insurance business is because the industry, although complex, is boring.

"The sector does not attract the same talent that the biotech or health care sectors do," he said. "It is not a glamorous place to be in the market."

To get up to speed on the insurance industry, Davis took courses at the College of Insurance in lower Manhattan.

"When I looked at the insurance industry, it sort of reminded me of the movie *It's a Wonderful Life*, where there was the Bailey Building and Loan and all they had was a liquidity problem but there was no fundamental business problem," he said. "I thought there was an enormous opportunity there."

Davis ultimately decided to join the family business when his grandfather, who had amassed a large portfolio of financial services stocks, started worrying about his own health. He was bequeathing it all to charity, but still was concerned about how the portfolio was going to be run and who would be running it.

"He was interested in having my father running the portfolio and my being involved in the process," Davis said. "So, we raised the issue of my coming to work with my dad. The trouble is that in cases like this you don't want to be employer of last resort."

Instead of sort of being a tagalong, Davis and his father decided that he should start his own fund. That would allow him to build his own record and be independent of the family but still be part of the organization.

"I felt that I needed a way to measure my own performance that was objective, separate and apart from the other portfolios," he said. "The whole idea of the nepotism issue was really important to me, and I needed to have my own track record and do something on my own."

Davis joined the firm, started the fund, and was also the analyst for the firm's New York Venture fund that his father was managing. This allowed him to have his own fund and sink or swim based on his own performance.

"I think it was absolutely critical at the time for both me and my father," he said. "I wanted to be able to look myself in the mirror and say, 'Okay, this is my record; I did this,' and my father wanted to be able to say, 'Well, there is the record, and it is better than New York Venture, and I have confidence in his ability.' "

While Davis could do his own thing in the firm, he was restricted to using the style in which the family built its fortune: no trading of futures, low turnover, and, most important, sticking with the family's unique way of picking stocks through fundamental analysis.

A key to the firm's success over the years is its culture of intellectual honesty. When you step off the elevator into its offices, you immediately see a wall filled with framed stock certificates—shares of companies the firm owns that have been successful. The certificates for the unsuccessful investments are also framed: They're hung on the wall above the watercooler to remind the investment team of its mistakes.

"One of the things that working for the church made relevant is a sort of idea or sense of stewardship about what we are doing," he said. "To that end it is very important to us how we communicate with our customers. In every letter to a shareholder we talk about our mistakes and explain what happened so that they know what is going on. We want to be able to look at ourselves in the mirror and be able to say that we delivered good results for the people who entrusted us with their money."

The firm currently manages about $35 billion through a number of vehicles that are part of the same pool of assets split among both load and no-load mutual funds and separate accounts. Slightly more than half the assets are in the mutual funds. Clients include insurance companies' variable annuities, as well as some managed money programs for wire houses (large brokerage firms like Salomon Smith Barney, UBS Paine Webber, and Morgan Stanley Dean Witter), endowments, and high-net-worth individuals. For the most part, the assets come in through brokers, financial planners, and consultants, although some come straight from investors.

"We prefer working through intermediaries, because customer service is a core competency that some firms have and that we do not. Our core competency is research, not taking calls and answering questions from investors," he said. "Most of the customers who come to us directly tend to be investors that do their own research. Because we don't advertise in the papers and we don't do television ads, we feel that if people find us, they have done their own research and are a better customer than somebody that was sold a bill of goods by an advertisement that promotes two-year performance."

More recently, though, potential investors have seen some advertisements in financial publications, which Davis finally agreed to. Even so, the Davis ads do not contain performance data or star ratings, unlike most mutual fund ads.

"The board [of directors] asked us to advertise, and the only way we agreed to do it was if we did it our way, which was to promote the investment philosophy of the firm and our style and strategy," he said.

Another thing that makes the Davis group of funds unique is the amount of money the employees, family, and outside directors have invested into the company's products. It amounts to just less than 10 percent of total assets. Because of this large concentration, the firm is very concerned with the type of investors it attracts.

"If we get people that move in and out of the funds, then that is going to hurt our existing shareholders because we are going to have to focus on managing cash instead of investors," he said.

To understand the Davis style is to understand that stocks are not just pieces of paper; they are ownership interests in businesses. So you need to forget the prices that wiggle around in the newspaper, the charts, the graphs, and the options, and focus solely on the business.

"It basically comes down to deciding what businesses you want to own. Our best customers tend to be people who have built up their own businesses and sold them, because they immediately say things like, 'You want to own businesses that have high return on capital,'" he said. "Most people think you can simply run a screen that tells you return on capital. When we hear that, our answer is always no—first of all, because you have to understand how much capital was actually deployed, and, second, you have to understand if the earnings are reflected in the return on capital, because you don't want to own businesses that are overleveraged."

The second part of the Davis style is to look at the company from a capitalist perspective.

"Once we determine that the business generates a high return on capital (and we live in a capitalist world where money flows to where returns are the highest), we want to figure out if those returns are sustainable," he said. "This part of the analysis is the competitive part of the analysis. We ask, who are the competitors, and are they getting better or worse, and will the business be able to continue to grow?"

To determine the company's competitive advantage, Davis and his team look first at its slice of the marketplace, the quality of its brands, and its distribution and international operations.

"Nobody will ever be able to duplicate McDonald's international operation and distribution, for example. The CEOs will be fired and turned over before the shareholders let them spend the money to develop that type of organization," he said. "I think the CEO of McDonald's once told me that the company lost money in Egypt for 13 years. I mean, what CEO can you go to today and say, 'I've got a great business but you are going to lose money for 13 years and then you are going to make a little.' Forget it. They will laugh you out of the room."

One thing that is really important to Davis is how the company views computer technology.

"Take, for example, *The World Book Encyclopedia*," he said. "[World Book, Inc.] had a great business model. Customers valued [the encyclopedia] and paid something like $500 for it while it cost $300 to produce. It had a good margin and a solid brand, which was a good deal for everybody. The problem was it was replaced by something that cost the end user $15, that was more user-friendly, and that cost 40 cents to stamp out."

Encarta, the Microsoft Corporation's product that Davis was talking about, came about when the software company purchased a third-tier supermarket encyclopedia publisher and offered such a compelling advance in the way people got information that it forever changed the encyclopedia industry.

"It is amazing that the business model of World Book, which was such a successful company for so long, became obsolete in two or three years because of technology," he said. "So you have got to study technology and understand how it is going to affect your business. If you own a newspaper, you'd better understand how eBay, Inc. is going to affect your classified business."

The third thing that Davis and his team look at is management.

"It seems that most of Wall Street is not concerned with who is running the business or who is going to be hired to run the business once management steps away," he said. "Because as an owner of a partial share of the business, you are going to have a partner who is going to run the business. You need to understand who managers are and how they are going to perform."

Davis said that in evaluating managers, he takes his cues from his grandfather's playbook. His grandfather believed managers were either doers or blockers. Doers aren't necessarily brilliant or great strategic visionaries or those with the best backgrounds, but they get the job done.

"They are people that you would want to be executor of your will or who you would be proud to have marry your daughter; that is the sort of person that you want to run your business," Davis said. "It all comes down to determining what sort of businesses you want to own, understanding how they operate, and understanding who is running the show."

Then there is the valuation. How much are you going to have to pay to acquire a piece of the business? Davis looks at the company's market capitalization and its debt and then studies and adjusts the balance sheet to arrive at a decision.

"When it comes to making a valuation, our insurance background comes in handy, because of our understanding of accounting methods on various industries," he said. "Take, for example, the Chicago Tribune Company. They used to say that they had a $9 billion market cap, but they had $2 billion after-tax of America Online stock. So if you wanted to buy the Tribune for the newspapers, the television [stations], the Cubs, and [its stake in] the WB [Television] network, you would have to back close to $3 billion out of the stock in order to put a valuation on it."

Davis said that once you determine a valuation, you need to look at what the business is earning today. To do that, look at its net operating profit after taxes, and then adjust it for the difference between depreciation and maintenance and capital spending, which may be much higher or much lower.

"Railroads, for example, have to spend more of their depreciation just to keep their lines running and to keep their trusses from falling down. That will lower their earnings, while other companies spend a fraction of their depreciation on maintenance, so you need to get a sense of that in order to make a decision," he said.

He also looks at noncash charges and adjusts for stock options to employees. The idea is to get a complete picture not only of where the earnings are coming from but also where they are going.

"One of the most unbelievable examples of the way options can affect a balance sheet was a situation with Donaldson, Lufkin & Jenrette. When the firm came public that first year, they had a very high compensation expense relative to the rest of the industry, and management promised to get it under control," he said. "Well, sure enough the next year came around and they had a relatively low compensation expense. Nobody got a pay cut, but because they were public they could give them all the financial equivalent in options, and because options expense does not appear on the financial statement, under GAAP [generally accepted accounting principles] rules, it did not impact the balance sheet.

"Obviously the profitability of DLJ did not change that much that year, but the GAAP earnings jumped up tremendously," he continued. "They did not do anything wrong, or anything that any other company doesn't, but we adjust for that. We look at how many of the shares are going to management, so that we can understand how much of a company we are going to own over time and how much of the upside we are going to participate in if management continues to give out stock."

The last question, which Davis says is the most important, hinges on understanding the difference between owning a share of the business and owning the whole of the business. The difference is that you do not get to decide what happens to the company and its earnings; management does. In the old days, management paid out earnings in dividends, but now they may invest in new businesses, buy back stock, or just let profits build up in a bank.

"They make all sorts of decisions as to what to do with that coupon, if you will, that the business provides," he said. "Over 10 years, the return on that reinvested earnings stream has got to be more significant than your starting point of how much earnings you are getting. If not, then the investment does not make sense."

Davis said investors should think about the company as if it were a bond. If you are paying 20 times earnings for that business, that is equivalent to a 5 percent coupon (the payment that a fixed income investment pays annually to the investor). But if that business is able to reinvest in buildings and factories so that it gets a 20 percent return on investment, then your coupon the next year is 5 percent plus the 20 percent return on the 5 percent that was reinvested. That means your yield is now 6 percent. The next year it will grow to 7.25 and then 8.5 and so on.

Alternatively, if you buy a business really cheaply, let's say at 10 times earnings, it may look great because it yields 10 percent. But the problem could be that management is not making good investments—in most cases, the investments are yielding 5 percent. Over time the initial 10 percent yields will go toward 5, and the investment will go nowhere but down.

"Even though the 10 may look cheaper, it ends up that the 20 with a 5 percent coupon is much cheaper and a better business, and it probably has a stronger management," he said. "We spend a lot of time on understanding the economics of a business, focusing on what the business is really earning and if the balance sheet really reflects appropriate values and how management is investing its capital."

It comes down to looking for the highest-quality businesses, with the best growth prospects, run by the best people, and with the highest coupon possible. While Davis will invest in almost every sector of the market, the key is that the companies have to pass through the firm's initial filter before they earn the right to be researched more thoroughly.

"We will look at anything, and we want to believe that the businesses we are going to invest in have good reinvestment characteristics or managements that are going to return money to shareholders," he said. "If you use those conditions, you are going to definitely weed out a lot of businesses. That's because there are lots of businesses that are crappy businesses that have managements who keep building crappy factories."

For the most part, Davis will hold stocks for years, versus other funds that hold stocks for only months or even days. In the best-case scenario, once Davis makes an investment, he would like to hold it forever. The reality, though, is that companies change.

"I think that we have some AIG [American International Group] stock that cost us 12 cents because we have owned it for so long, and, obviously, the longer we can own a business the better," he said. "Owning something longer allows us to have the opportunity to get not only the earnings growth of the business but, over time, a revaluation of that earnings stream."

"My grandfather called these types of investments growth stocks in disguise," Davis continued. "He said that you wanted to buy these types of companies whether they are disguised as cyclical companies, dull financial companies, or boring businesses, but as long as you could find a company with growth in the earnings it made sense to look at it further."

Davis found that his investment in AIG provided him not only a 15 percent earnings growth rate, bringing a fourfold increase in earnings over 10 years, but also a price-to-earnings ratio that went from 12 to 30.

"You've got a stock price that went up fourfold and earnings that tripled, so you end up making 12 times on your money," he said. "That is the best of both worlds, something we call a double play."

Davis said that by sticking to its discipline, the firm tends to eliminate stocks with very, very high price-to-earnings ratios. If you buy shares of a company with a P/E of 50, he noted, then the stock is going to have to go up 50 percent and keep going up 50 percent a number of times before its coupon crosses the risk-free rate of return found in the bond market.

"It can happen, and some companies with no earnings do make it. It is like owning a zero coupon bond, but with owning a zero coupon bond you must understand the credit quality behind it and what is eventually going to give you those earnings," he said.

Yet Davis and his team will occasionally invest in high price-to-earnings ratio companies, but they really have to understand the business and where it is going before they do.

Take, for example, the wireless phone industry, in particular cellular phone service licenses. Davis knew that initially the licensees had no earnings. Still, he believed after researching the industry that it was virtually inevitable that they would earn something, and in this case it turned out that they earned quite a lot.

To find companies that meet the firm's investment criteria, the team members look at everything they can to get information on a particular business. They want to know how it's operating, who its management is, how strong its model is, and where it expects to go. They also look at regulatory filings and talk to suppliers and competitors.

First they cull a list of businesses they think they want to invest in. Then they try to estimate a fair value for each company—which is generally a wide range, depending how well they know the business, but never wider than, say, 50 percent above and below what the stock is trading at. For example, Davis' fair value for American Express Company is anywhere from $25 to $50 a share. Some people may think that means that he does not know the company very well, but what really matters to him is believing in the math that established the fair value range.

Davis told a story about Ben Graham when I asked him to explain his definition of fair value. Graham had one of his students try to find a fair value for a company by looking at five years' worth of data. The result was something like a fair value range of between $26 and $105 a share. While some thought the information was useless, Graham said it was enormously valuable. If the nature of the market is to go to extremes, by comparing the data to the current price, you will find that 98 percent of those companies will be in the fair value range most of the time, while 2 percent will not. Keep watching, he said, because over time something will cause some to drop below the range, and that is when you have to buy.

This led us to Davis' story about Costco Wholesale Corporation, the warehouse retailer.

"We always liked Costco—great business, fanatical management, the model works," he said. "It was at $34 or $35 per share, outside our range of fair value, so we sat and watched it. It went to $40, then $45, then $50, and we were patient. We stayed on top of it, and in the summer of 2000 we finally got our chance. The company announced that they were going to have a shortfall for a number of factors, and the stock opened lower, well within our fair value band, and we finally got a chance to buy it. That day we became the largest shareholder in the company."

Davis said that his team bought the stock at a low of $27 and rode it up to $45 and back down to about $33 when we met in mid-September of 2001.

"Even though the stock has clearly come off its high, it is

still pretty satisfying owning the company. There are not many stocks that have increased over the last 12- or 15-month period," he said.

The fair value strategy works the other way, too. If a stock Davis owns goes through the high range of the fair value band, he sells it and waits for it to drop below the band before getting in again.

"That is what happened in the technology area. We sort of got in at the low end, and as soon as the stocks started pushing through the fair value band we became very big sellers," he said. "One of the reasons our performance was so strong in 2000 was because we sold so much technology, but in retrospect it was never *enough*!"

When we met, just days after the World Trade Center disaster, one of the stocks that Davis and his team liked was American Express, and while the market as a whole seemed to think that it was not a good play, they disagreed.

"All of the problems and issues with the company are out on the table, and it is pretty obvious that it is going to get a lot worse before it gets better," he said. "But we also bought Wells Fargo and Citibank in the wake of the real estate crisis in the early 1990s. We had a sense of, well, this situation could go on for another two years and when they come out the other side they could be selling for six times earnings. Well, the situation with American Express could go on for another two years and they could be selling at 14 times earnings. That's a reasonable price for American Express, but it is not a giveaway."

Davis was buying the stock at around $25 a share on the day we met and planning to buy more if it continued to fall. On the day I wrote this part of the book, the stock closed at $29.06.

Davis' goal is not to be optimized in one part of the cycle but to perform over the entire cycle. That means, he said, "that every single year we get criticized for looking either too much like a growth manager or too much like a value manager."

He continued, "Our answer is simple. We say, 'Look, our board judges us on a rolling 10-year performance versus the S&P 500, and in every 10-year period since 1969 we have beaten this standard.' What we tell people is that they should invest with Janus or they should invest with us, and they say, 'What do you mean? You are at opposite ends of the spectrum.' Our reply is, 'As long as you have conviction and are willing to ride the up cycles and the down cycles, you will do just as well with either of us.' "

In the end, Davis' comments echo those of other managers in these pages: The key to success in picking either mutual funds or individual stocks is conviction. Unless you have conviction in what you are doing, you will not be successful.

"You shouldn't buy a mutual fund—or a stock, for that matter—because your neighbors have told you how much money they have made in it. By that time it is too late," he said.

Davis feels that his goal for the firm is like his father's. He hopes that 30 years from now he can look in the mirror and say that he did the best he could for the investors who gave him money to manage.

"By recognizing our weaknesses and basically understanding what we stink at and adding people who can compensate for these weaknesses," he says, "we will be able to reach this goal and in turn have many satisfied investors. That, in turn, will mean we have done something worthwhile."

What I Think . . .

Talk about having big shoes to fill! Imagine the pressure for success when you are the third generation to run a business. Many would crack under the pressure. Not Chris Davis. He's shown that he can fill the family shoes quite well, thank you. He really seems to understand money management and how to build successful portfolios. I believe a lot of it has to do with the fact that successful money management is coursing through his veins. The fact that he really seems to be enjoying himself doesn't hurt much, either.

Of all the people I met with for this book, Davis seems to be having the most fun at his job. And fun, as we all know, is very important to success. I'm not saying that the others don't enjoy their work; it's just that he enjoys it the most. That's what sets him apart from the rest of the pack.

So there you have it: 11 mutual fund managers (one a team) that each bring something unique to the business. I hope you found the profiles interesting as well as informative and learned something not only about the way these people manage money but also about the people themselves. As I said earlier, you can never have too much information when it comes to anything, let alone your investments. The more you know, the better decisions you can make.

From reading the profiles, many of you may have come to the conclusion that while the managers are different on the surface, underneath they're all the same. They all try to understand a company inside and out, they all rely on fundamental analysis, and they all focus on long-term gains, not just the ends of their noses.

I came to this same conclusion from interviewing them and spending time learning about how they operate on a day-to-day basis. I'm sure that many of you think that it's all rather simple: You look at a universe of companies, find one that is excelling or poised to excel in its particular industry, buy the stock, then wait. Well, not really. If it were that easy, everyone would be doing it—and doing it successfully.

Managers try to make it look easy. They're paid to instill in their investors the confidence that the manager has the skills, the ability, and the wherewithal to beat the market. Your job as an investor is to see through the marketing material and get to the heart of the matter.

The managers profiled in this book offer investments that are unique in today's marketplace. Each was singled out for a distinct style and strategy. While many may follow similar principles and use similar tools, each brings a different approach to money management and to the investment process.

Today's marketplace offers more than 10,000 mutual funds. More than half call themselves growth or value funds, and another third call themselves sector funds, so it was very difficult to choose from all these just 11 to be profiled.

The process, while not completely scientific, was built around the idea that all investment portfolios, regardless of size or duration, should consist of at least one growth fund, one value fund, and three sector funds. Call it Strachman's theory on portfolio diversification, or what have you; I believe it's the right number of funds for an investor. The idea is to create a portfolio with as little overlap (funds that own the same stocks) as possible. That's often hard to do in today's crowded marketplace.

There is likely to be little or no overlap in a portfolio consisting of five funds, one investing in, say, growth stocks, another in value stocks, the third in biotech and health care stocks, the fourth in financial services, and the fifth in energy and natural resources stocks. Conversely, a portfolio of five growth funds or five value funds, all investing in largely the same stocks, is most likely not the right combination for long-term success.

Many investors are looking for more than a list of good growth fund managers or sector managers. They're searching for information to help them to make better decisions, so the hardest part of this exercise came when I had to single out the 11 managers.

The two characteristics most important to this part of the research were assets under management and time in the money management business. It is important to use managers who have been at the helm for more than three years. While some think it's great to chase the hot new managers, I don't. And as for size, it is my belief—something that I practice as well as preach—that large funds don't offer as good an opportunity as smaller ones.

So, where do you go from here? Well, the first thing you need to do is to look at each of the managers and understand what he or she brings to the table.

I want to make it very clear that I am not recommending that you invest with any of the managers unless you do research and come to that conclusion on your own. The information on the previous pages is just a guideline and should be just one piece of the research you do before investing. What I have written is what I believe, but remember that it's only one man's opinion and that if I didn't like the way the managers operate, I wouldn't have included them in the first place.

For the past eight or so years, I've dedicated a good portion of my life to meeting with money managers and understanding how they think and work and, most importantly, manage money. I have met a lot of people for whom I have enormous respect and many others for whom I have little or no respect. The problem, of course, is telling the good from the bad.

Numbers never lie, some people say, so performance is the only way. I think that's true on some level, but it's only part of the puzzle. It comes down to people. The really important thing is to understand the person "pulling the trigger," making the investment decision and in turn allocating the assets. I think that over the long term the managers profiled in these pages are some of the best and brightest minds in the business.

★ *chapter four* ★

RESOURCES

The idea behind this book is to make investors understand that no matter how smart, well intentioned, and self-confident they are, the only way to be successful in the market is to use investment professionals. The corollary to this premise is that, more often than not, picking individual stocks will not work over the long term.

Investment professionals concentrate all their energy on managing portfolios. Remember that your portfolio is important, it is real, and it is something you need to take seriously. Chasing tips or what you believe is the next great thing is no different from going to Las Vegas and putting all your chips on black. Actually, you might even think about doing that. Going to Vegas is a lot of fun and, in some cases, can be very rewarding both financially and spiritually. Still, gambling with your portfolio isn't a good idea. If you insist on doing it, put this book down and call a travel agent. You'll probably have more fun and could potentially make or lose as much money as you would by chasing the next hot tip.

To determine how to manage your portfolio, you need first to determine the level of risk you are willing to tolerate and how long you have before you'll need the money you're investing. To keep from boring those who already know what their goals are and have an idea about what they want to invest in, I will just say this to those who don't: Find someone you can trust and respect. Discuss your situation. Then devise a goal, come up with a plan, and begin to execute it.

Investing and investment planning are a constant learning experience, and you should treat them as such. The next few pages will show you what I believe are good places to find information that will both give you tools to understand investment strategy and, more important, provide you with a steady stream of data to make you a smarter investor.

Most people think that higher returns mean a more successful investment. Sure, high returns are good, but to determine the actual success of the investment you need to understand both the risk involved and the loss you would have incurred if the investment had gone south instead of north. Everybody has different definitions of success. What one investor views as *Nirvana* another might see as the *Titanic*.

What I want is a return somewhere between 8 and 15 percent annually, net of fees. That means what I actually get after the investment manager or brokerage firm takes its slice. The net number is very important, and you need to look at it in all cases.

I am sure some readers at this point are saying 8 to 15 percent is too low and that they were looking for something more like 20 or 30 percent a year. I don't think that it is realistic or sustainable. Like all of you, I would very much like to have investments bring in that much each year, but the likelihood of consistently posting those numbers is very small. And 8 to 15 percent a year is what I am looking for over the long haul, counting bad years as well as good (i.e., an average of about 11.5 percent).

Besides, anyone who would like to see what 11.5 percent annual growth would do to a modest investment portfolio of, say, $25,000 over 10 years should go to www.bloomberg.com or www.moneycentral.msn.com and run the numbers in one of their compounding programs. You might be amazed at how fast the nest egg grows in a relatively short period of time.

The baseball maxim that those who try to hit home runs all the time end up striking out more often than they hit the ball out of the park applies to investing, too.

Many investors don't want to believe this, for the same reason most mutual fund managers don't know how to short the market: It is counter to the American way. We all believe that we are at least as smart as the next guy if not more so. Sure, there are the Einsteins and Salks and Freuds and Edisons with unique levels of intellect and vision. Leaving those couple of hundred people aside, when it comes to investing, all of us think we are smarter than everybody else.

Even though you may be as intelligent as the people who manage money and pick stocks all day long, you don't. That's why they have an edge—an edge that you can't even appreciate because you don't know how it affects your level of success in the market. Fear not, however, because there is something you can do that will help level the playing field: You can educate yourself.

You took the first step by buying this book and trying to understand how 11 money managers actually manage money. I applaud you, and I hope that you found the book helpful so far. Still, your education shouldn't end when you finish the last page. It should be a constant journey, part of your everyday life. Set aside an hour or even a half hour every day to read the business pages, to surf the Web, or to read another book. It is important to stay up-to-date, aware, and informed. The next few pages will help you do this. This is not a personal finance book, so subjects like credit card debt, mortgages, insurance, and so forth aren't covered. There are many places to find information on these subjects, and if you need help (all of us do), then I suggest you look at your local bookstore for a short but simple book on personal finance.

Many people believe that the explosion of Internet, print, and broadcast news outlets focusing on the markets has helped to level the playing field for individual investors. It has, but it is causing a lot of problems as well. Because there is so much market information, it is hard to separate the good from the bad. And if the field is level, with everybody seeing the same information, how is anyone ever going to find unique opportunities? Remember, all of us can walk onto the field at Fenway Park, but few of us can hit a pitch thrown by Pedro Martinez.

To help you at least know what Pedro—or the market—is throwing at you, here are the places that many others and I find most useful. There is nothing personal or sinister about the list, and I am sure there are many fine outlets that I am leaving off it.

Remember that most people who live by the ticker die by the ticker. Stand clear of them; you will only lose money.

Also, be careful about overdosing. For some reason (I blame the media), it seems that everywhere you turn there is a story about the markets or investing. Our nation has been consumed by the bull (and now bear) markets of the past five years. I would like to propose that bars, restaurants, and other public places be prohibited from tuning their TVs to financial news programs. You know something is wrong with the world when you go into a barbershop and everyone is watching a Saturday edition of *Wall Street Week* instead of a college football game.

And now the list.

The Internet

Twenty years ago it would have been very hard to find a person outside Wall Street who could tell you how to find stock quotes other than the prices printed in the daily newspaper. Today anyone who wants them can get live quotes delivered almost anywhere almost instantaneously.

Over the past five years or so, the use of the Internet has exploded. For a while it seemed that everybody was starting a web site that offered discount brokerage, investment advice, and tools to give people a leg up on the professionals. Unfortunately, when the Internet bubble burst some good companies folded or merged out of existence, leaving would-be investors out in the cold. Fortunately, next to pornography, financial sites are the most profitable on the Web, and there is no lack of sites to click onto.

The Internet is a great place to start your journey. There are a lot of very good sites out there that provide the right kind of information to make you a smarter and better investor. The problem is finding a way to cut through the noise. While the number of financial web sites is large, most of them provide the same old thing. The only difference is the packaging. The truth is that you don't need live stock quotes unless you are day trading. If you are using the money managers in this book or ones like them, their net asset values come out sometime after 6 P.M. daily, so it makes no sense to subscribe to live pricing services. What you do need are a few sites that provide you with unique views on what's happening. Then you can disregard all of the other sites.

Here are the sites that I use and why I like them. In each case, except where specified, I look at or get e-mail updates from the sites throughout the day.

Yahoo! Finance

Yahoo! Finance (http://finance.yahoo.com) is a great site. It provides everything you need for a basic education about a stock or mutual fund in an easy-to-use and easy-to-navigate group of pages. I use this site every day—most days three or four times. I particularly like the ability to customize the site to make it your home page. While this feature is available on most web sites, it really works well here. The site allows you to set up the page so it has everything you need in one place. It takes some time to set it up and get it working the way you want—the setup can be somewhat frustrating—but in the end it's worth it.

I particularly like the news tracker feature. It allows you to program in a list of words (say, manager's names, topics, or phrases), and daily the site provides news stories in which the words appear. For example, you can have it track the words "mutual fund" or "Strachman," and it will list news stories in which the subject appears. This can really come in handy.

Another feature of the site that I think is very important is the Worldinvestorlink.com function. This service allows you to download a prospectus, annual report, or other pertinent information about a stock or mutual fund almost instantaneously.

I think Yahoo! Finance should the first layer of concrete in your educational foundation. While a lot of people think the pages are too basic, I think they work great. On top of that, the site is totally free.

Bloomberg.com

Bloomberg.com should be the next layer of your foundation. I believe there has never been and never will be a better place to get news and information about the markets. Everything you could possibly need to know about a company and its financials is available on this system. Most of us can't afford to have a Bloomberg terminal at home, and going to the web site (www.bloomberg.com) is the next best thing.

It is an all-in-one site that has everything you need and more. I particularly like its news-and-information component. Its reporters are usually first to break a story, and its editors are able to disseminate the information efficiently and succinctly. Their reporters tend to be the scrappiest—a good thing—whether it be on the Net, in print, or on broadcasts, but there are better places to find the second-day stories that usually provide a much more thorough level of information. It's important to realize this weakness.

Still, this is the site to go to for analytical data, especially rankings. Their Web people have thought of everything when it comes to slicing and dicing topics. I especially like their mutual fund ranking pages and the ability to search for data on money managers.

One thing that Bloomberg.com does better than the rest is to make it easy to get around the site. Ease of use is the key, and their people have mastered it.

TheStreet.com

If Yahoo! provides basic news and information and Bloomberg provides basic news and analytics, you're still missing market commentary and actual investment advice. For this I turn to TheStreet.com (www.thestreet.com), where I find interesting commentary about the market and what makes it tick, literally. The people at TheStreet.com have found columnists who write interesting stories that provide readers with a unique view of what is and what is not important. Their columns are witty, smart, and intelligently written. I believe that they have cornered the market on columnists who provide a view of Wall Street and how it operates unlike any other site out there. I will say, however, that one or two individuals appear to be nothing more than media hounds and just like to hear themselves speak, and I would steer clear of their columns. For the most part, though, the copy is definitely worth reading.

On the downside, getting around the site isn't easy, and it's sometimes quite difficult to separate all the noise from the music. Still, once you do, you'll realize why the site is important and you'll constantly turn to its pages in search of the latest column. Once you find a column that you like, I highly suggest that you bookmark it so you can quickly and easily find it again.

Morningstar.com

For raw mutual fund data, and the most basic information on funds, fund complexes, and fund managers, this web site (www.morningstar.com) is the place to go.

The problem is that the good stuff costs. While some people, including yours truly, pay for access to the premium information, which includes in-depth analysis and commentary on funds and fund complexes, it would be a waste of money for anyone who is not really going to use it. I guess that's true with everything. In this case, though, it's important to actually use what you got, as my father would say. If you do, then it will be worth every bit of the expense. Even if you aren't going to buy the premium service, the site still offers some good information free and it is definitely worth checking out.

Another drawback to the site is the lack of frequent updating. It is my experience that most of the fund data, including top 10, performance, assets under management, and in some cases even the names of mutual fund managers, aren't up-to-date. That's a problem.

Google.com

If there's a better search engine on the Web than Google.com, I'd like someone to tell me about it. I absolutely love this site (www.google.com). It is easy, it is to the point, and it works.

Type in a phrase, keyword, or subject, and in about 30 seconds (depending on the speed of your Internet connection) you get an answer. That's it. The folks at Google.com understand the principle of KISS (keep it simple, stupid), and we all benefit from it. It is a great site to find information on a manager or an investment style or strategy. I use it daily and find it to be an indispensable tool in researching not only investment ideas and subjects but everything else as well. I wish everything on the Internet worked as well—life would be a lot simpler.

Print Media

Once you have mastered the Internet for minute-by-minute news and information, you need to step back and look at print publications. It is here where you will truly expand your knowledge.

I believe in print. Sure, some people say that in today's technologically advanced society print is dead, but I'm not one of them. Reading the news on the Web is great for the quick hits, but when it comes to reading the whole story, I like to be able to hold something in my hand.

Over the past five or six years, so many publications have started and so many of the old standbys (the names should roll off your tongue) have redesigned their business news coverage to combat the Internet that it seems there are just too many places to turn.

This is a good thing. As we all know, competition makes organizations stronger and more effective. We all benefit from this new level of competition.

Newspapers

A journalism professor once told me that I should read the *New York Times* so that I would always have something to talk about at cocktail parties. Well, that was in the early 1990s. I think that if I spoke with him today he would suggest some of the publications listed here. That's not because the *Times* has become irrelevant (perish the thought!) but because the market looks to be the topic du jour for some time to come.

Investor's Business Daily

This is a great tool. The idea behind the publication is to provide a unique insight into the markets' workings, and it does it every time. The stories are thorough, accurate, and to the point. Most of the stories it runs will not appear in other business publications, and that is what gives the paper its edge. It seems that its editors understand their strengths and weaknesses, as well as what they are supposed to do. They leave nonessential market, business, and other news reporting to other publications.

I really like this newspaper and believe that anyone interested in learning about investing and companies should turn to it regularly.

Financial Times

The people at the *Financial Times* seem to understand what is and what isn't important when it comes to covering business. They have a unique way of cutting through the clutter that is today's global marketplace to write stories that make sense.

The *FT*'s strength is that, unlike other financial newspapers, it takes a global view of the markets. Over the past year or so it has expanded its coverage of the markets, and in particular money managers, making it an even more important tool of the well-informed. While the *FT* and the *Journal* may have similar stories, the *FT* seems to hit the mark better. That may be because it's owned by a stodgy British publishing company and printed on salmon-colored newsprint, but whatever the reason, you will truly be well-informed once you get into the habit of reading this paper.

Barron's

The information that the people at this newspaper put out is priceless. Not only is their hard news accurate and informative, but also, like TheStreet.com, the editors at *Barron's* have found some of the best and brightest market commentators around. There are few Saturday mornings that I don't sit down with a large pot of coffee and read *Barron's* cover to cover. There is always something interesting in its pages. What makes it indispensable is the simple fact that it does what it does well.

I particularly like its question-and-answer pieces. While I am usually not a big fan of Q&As and often find them boring, *Barron's* seems much livelier than most. It has to do with the editorial process—a process *Barron's* does quite well.

Magazines

There are probably as many magazines covering personal finance, investing, the market, and business as there are magazines covering food and automobiles. The problem is how to decide what not to read. While some new titles seem to be doing a good job, I like the older ones. For some reason, they carry better-written, better-researched, and more thoroughly thought-out articles than the new publications. None of the names on the list should surprise.

Forbes

Forbes is the place to start. Although I don't always agree with the angles its editors take or some of the subjects they cover, for the most part they do a good job providing stories that make me think—and that's what's important. Their stories are neat and never too long. For the most part, its staff doesn't write stories just for the sake of writing them, as some other publications do, and that is to their credit.

It seems that in the past couple of years *Forbes* has started to be a little more sensational in covering Wall Street, and that may be what gives it its edge. I really enjoy reading the magazine. One of the things that makes it so attractive is its format. The stories are quick and to the point, and I don't feel that the writers are talking down to me. I hate a magazine that thinks it is better than its readers.

The problem is that sometimes its editors miss the point. One recent story in particular did readers an injustice. Frankly, I was embarrassed for the editors. (Anyone interested can e-mail me at strach@mindspring.com, and I will tell you more.) Still, *Forbes* does it well overall, and it's a publication that you need to read. *Forbes* has a number of supplements that are also very good reading, and you should check them out, as well.

Fortune

In fairness to my friends at *Fortune* (and there are a few), I will say that the only reason I put *Forbes* ahead of *Fortune* is because of the alphabet. I really like this magazine. It has such a good staff of writers, reporters, and editors, many of whom have been around so long that they define what makes a good business journalist.

The articles in the magazine are so thorough that when I finish reading I feel as if I were in the room with the writer. I never miss an issue, because when it comes to overall business information nobody covers the topics as well as *Fortune*. I would almost say it does everything right, but, frankly, nobody can do *everything* right. *Fortune* is really worth subscribing to.

SmartMoney

There are few magazines that cover personal finance, including investing, as well as *SmartMoney*. The folks there seem to understand that not everyone is a millionaire, that not everyone is a rocket scientist, and that people are in search of good basic information to make them better investors. I like the style of the stories and find them very informative. The companion web site (www.smartmoney.com) is also a bonus, and you should use it in conjunction with the print version. This is not true of the *Forbes* or *Fortune* web sites, which add little if any value.

The editors have a good grasp of current topics and make things easy to understand. Usually the magazine's year-end and New Year's issues are very thorough and thought provoking.

They really should not be missed for tax and estate planning advice. Nevertheless, when it comes to dissecting money managers or providing trading or investment style and strategy stories, there are better places to turn to.

BusinessWeek

Unlike the magazines mentioned previously, *BusinessWeek* is a news publication, more like *Barron's* than, say, *Forbes* or *Fortune*. And while some may think that its news is dated or just not news, I always find something interesting or important in its pages.

The problem is that you have actually to read each page. Most people, myself included, tend to flip through the pages of a publication and look at one thing while skipping another. Well, it is my experience that doesn't work with *BusinessWeek*; you actually have to read it all. So if you're going to be lazy, save your money.

Obviously I have left many web sites, newspapers, and magazines off my list. I hope writers and editors don't feel slighted. I am sure that many people are surprised that I didn't include the *Wall Street Journal* and the *New York Times*. Believe me, I think these are important publications, and I read them every day. But everyone knows their strengths. I believe that more people need to understand the strengths of the *Financial Times* and *Investor's Business Daily*.

There are many other good financial news publications that I look at from time to time. The ones I listed, though, are the ones I read most often and so feel most comfortable recommending to you.

If you think there is a something I overlooked, please send me an e-mail (strach@mindsping.com), and we can discuss it. I am always interested in finding new resources. Time is the only true commodity we have, and we need to use it wisely.

Books

I've designed the resource guide to help you find news and information to make you better investors, but one thing that I haven't covered is your basic education. As I mentioned earlier, this book is just one of many that you will need to read in order to make informed investment decisions. It provides a good foundation of understanding "what works on Wall Street," but a foundation is just the beginning. You need to build upon the information you garnered from these pages and go forth into the bookstores and find other tools to make your education complete.

There are so many business and finance books out there that it would be impossible to put together a list that does the industry justice. Still, there are five books that I think everyone interested in investing should own and read with some regularity. Again, my apologies to those whose books I've left off. Come on, it's only one list. I'm sure that if your books are any good they will be on other people's lists.

One of the first ones you need to buy is *The Wall Street Journal Guide to Understanding Money & Markets* (HarperInformation, 1989). It's fun to read and easy to understand and a book that I find myself turning to time and again when I have a question or need to understand something. Some people may think that the book is too basic, but I don't agree. I think it does what it does well, and that is what is most important. Simple is always better, in my opinion.

Another must-have book is *The Wall Street Journal Guide*

to Understanding Personal Finance (Simon & Schuster, 3d ed., 2000). This book lays it all on the line again in a simple, easy-to-understand format that makes sense. I think that it covers personal finance and beginning investing better than any other book.

For those who call themselves investors (i.e., most of the readers of this book), another must-read is *Security Analysis: The Classic 1934 Edition*, by Benjamin Graham and David L. Dodd (McGraw-Hill, 1996). There is no better book than this for learning how to analyze stocks and how to understand the investment process. No library is complete without Graham and Dodd's bible. Many think it is dry and some call it outdated, but if you are really serious about investing, you are doing yourself an injustice by not taking the time to read it. Selecting securities is the most important part of the investment process, and this is the most important book written on the subject.

Barron's Educational Series' *Dictionary of Business Terms* (3d ed., 2000) is not something you just read; it is something you use. This is a tool that not only gives you definitions, but also explains concepts and brings things down to the most basic level. One of Wall Street's great myths is that things are hard to understand and just too complicated for the average person. Well, with this dictionary you will quickly realize just how smart you are and how simple Wall Street really is.

Reminiscences of a Stock Operator by Edwin Lefèvre (John Wiley & Sons, 75th anniversary ed., 1997) was one of the first books I read when I decided to leave my career as a journalist and work on Wall Street. It is the fictionalized biography of Jesse Livermore, tape reader, trader, and speculator extraordinaire. It is a fabulous book that will both help you understand the markets better and also teach you something about yourself. It's a wonderful read that shouldn't be missed by anyone who has any interest in Wall Street, money management, or investing.

Using the tools described in these pages should make you a better, smarter, and more thorough investor. If you realize that you don't know everything and can always learn something, then you are already succeeding where most people fail. Making money is not easy; if it was, everybody would be doing it.

★ *chapter five* ★

CONCLUSION

"To invest or not to invest?" That is the question that most people have been asking in the wake of the collapse of the stock market over the past couple of years.

And while there is a lot of hemming and hawing about what to do, the obvious answer is to invest.

No matter how far down the market has fallen or how low stock prices have gone, there is always an opportunity to make money from investing.

When people heard that I was writing a book on stock picking strategies, they immediately began asking me for tips. After all, the markets were falling and the end seemed nowhere in sight, so they wanted to know what these money managers knew that they did not.

It was almost laughable, because just 10 months earlier many of these same people would have said, "Oh, writing that is a waste. The market just keeps going up. We don't need professionals."

So what changed, and why did things get so bad? These are questions that the professionals and the academics will be looking for answers to for years to come. People will revisit the initial public offering explosion, the Internet craze, and everything else that they believe might have contributed to the massive losses that investors around the globe experienced in the wake of the bull that was the market.

The problem is, or was, that throughout the most recent bull market, everybody seemed to forget the fundamentals. They also forgot that stocks can and do go down.

I believe that once investors realize that stocks don't always go up, that there is something called volatility, that picking stocks is harder than taking a tip from a friend or finding the next great thing, then they should be able to weather the storm, and, what is more important, to be better, smarter, and wealthier investors.

That is the message of this book, which I hope is clear.

The key to being a successful stock picker is not finding something quickly that works and loading up on it; it is the exact opposite. It is first finding things that *don't* work and avoiding them, and then from that point on determining what will work and loading up on that.

"Many people think that it is easy to find investment opportunities, especially in light of the tech explosion that made everybody market mavens," said one manager who asked not to be identified. "The truth is that it is very hard, but, because people think it is easy, they try to do it themselves. Sometimes they make money and sometimes they lose, but I bet in the end they lose more often than they win. It is not a game; it is a business just like anything else, and people need to respect it as such."

Every successful stock picker is like a general who guides troops into a series of battles. Generals know that they need to win battle after battle and that they have to fight as hard as they can to achieve victory. They also know that each battle is not the last time that they are going to fight, and therefore they need to keep something in reserve to be strong enough to fight another day.

All the people in this book, and I would venture to guess most of the money managers on the Street, would agree that in the long run a significant portion of their success comes by implementing capital preservation strategies. And just as a good general keeps some troops in reserve, ready for the next day, a good money manager always keeps some cash on the side for the next good idea to come along.

The most important lesson anyone can learn from reading any investment book is that to truly be successful, you must preserve your capital.

The preservation of capital should be the cornerstone of any solid money management program for institutional and retail investors alike. While the words are simple and the concept is easy to understand, retail investors all too often ignore it.

"People don't realize how hard it is to preserve capital," said Paul Wong, manager of Edgehill Capital, a hedge fund in Greenwich, Connecticut. "It is difficult because when you get a good idea that you think is going to run, you want to get the most out of it. Keeping cash on the side does not allow you to really do that. But you always need something on the side, so that when new ideas come along you can execute on them."

He continued, "What makes it even harder is once the idea starts to run, and you start making money, you begin to question how much you invested and why you did not put more into the position. Then you really get confused. But if you stick to your plan and execute it thoroughly, you will end up not second-guessing yourself. Instead you will be happy with the returns and move on to the next opportunity."

The profiles in the previous chapters illustrate that what seems to work on Wall Street is consistency, conviction, and patience. Fundamental analysis—determining the strength and weakness of a business, understanding whether it creates value, and evaluating its management—is what you need to look at when picking both stocks and investment managers.

The next great thing is fine, but it isn't worth chasing unless you get in and out quickly enough to avoid getting hurt. And because the next great thing is a fad, it is too hard to predict when the right time to get in and out might be.

Remember the "Baby on Board" signs in car windows? It was a fad that came and went before anyone knew it. Sure, some people made money in the beginning, but think of all the stores that got stuck with those little yellow signs in inventory. What a waste!

Scott Black summed it up best when he said, "People aren't interested in what I do, because it is not exciting." Investing should not be exciting. If you want excitement with your money, go to the casino. Investing is work, and it is not always fun.

As Black pointed out, talking about the stock of a company that made a lot of free cash or had no debt was of no interest to investors during the most recent bull market. Instead, the excitement was in stocks with lots of debt, that generated no cash, and that had little if any business model. While it worked in the short term, in the end a lot of people were burned badly. Did you ever hear of Qualcomm, Global Crossing, or Avanex?

"People forgot about fundamentals," one market commentator said. "They forgot about businesses and the strengths of management; they just chased returns that were not real."

Most people would agree that never before in the history of the world did anyone experience more excitement, more thrills, or higher returns than those that the most recent bull market showed to investors. This newfound euphoria made people crazy—crazy, like the people of Holland who thought the market for tulips was going to climb on and on forever.

Many people believed that the market would never give back its gains; they started giving up their day jobs and doing some other pretty foolish things to get into the game of buying and selling stocks.

I will never forget the day I was sitting in my office at the small money management firm where I worked when a colleague came in to tell me of the latest and greatest idea he had to make money.

He was going to liquidate his individual retirement accounts, take the penalty, and put the money to work by trading the market.

"I should be able to double or even triple it easily," he told me as I looked at him in disbelief. "It is like taking candy from a baby—everything is working, and I think in a few months I will probably have enough to quit my day job and focus on it full-time."

I could not believe it. I told him how silly it was and that he was making a big mistake. He just sort of shook his head in disagreement.

What got me even more was that here we were working for a professional money management firm, and one of the key employees was willing to become a day trader. It really made no sense—if he didn't want to have money at the firm, then why should anyone else?

Still, this is just one story of many during this unique period of the market. While some people clearly made a lot of money day trading, and there is a lot of merit to going that route, for the most part only the brokerage firms that supported these efforts made any money. The following are some stories about day traders that I think are important.

In early 1999, Eric* was working at a well-known law firm in New York City and decided that being a lawyer was no longer for him. Regardless of the fact that he made a good living and that he was on track to becoming a partner, he decided to chase his dream—or what he thought was his dream—of being a day trader.

Originally his dream had been to be a lawyer, but the bull market changed all that when in late 1998 a stock he bought tripled in three days. He decided he needed to get into the game and left the law firm to embark on his new career.

At first it was very exciting. He went to work at a famous day trading firm in lower Manhattan, took a seat at a trading turret, was taught how to use the trading system, and just like that, good-bye, lawyer; hello, day trader.

Eric thought it was strange that the only "training" the firm provided was teaching him how to use its order execution system and to read prices off the computer screen. When it came to learning basics, if there are such things as basics in the day trading business, the knowledge came from looking over other people's shoulders.

Initially he lost money. He estimated that in the first month he lost $10,000, and by the end of his first quarter of trading he had lost close to $28,000.

"In the beginning the losses really started to pile up, and it gets pretty nerve-racking, especially when you sit next to guys

*The names of individuals in this section have been changed at their request.

who are making $5,000 or $10,000 a day," Eric said. "For every trade I made money on, there were 5 or 10 that I lost money on, but after a while things started to click and the money started to roll in.

"Some of the guys let me watch what they were doing, and slowly I began to pick things up here and there, and finally I got the hang of it," he continued. "I learned how it worked, and it became profitable."

It really started to work for him. Some days he would make $1,000 to $2,000. On his best day ever he cleared $10,000. To him it was the sign that he had made it, that he had arrived as a day trader.

For some time Eric's "system," if you will, of extracting quick profits seemed to be working well. But in March 2000 everything seemed to stop. Instead of making daily profits, he started racking up daily losses. His system was no longer working, and neither was anyone else's at the firm, from what he could gather.

Even some of the senior people at the firm, the people who had been profiled in the mainstream business publications for the alleged millions that they made day trading, could not break even.

"When I got to the firm, one of the big traders was making about $200,000 a month," Eric said. "He was sort of the envy of everyone at the firm, but when the market turned and the Nasdaq crumbled, he stopped making money and started losing. His losses amounted to quite a bit of money. At some point in early 2001, he stopped trading altogether and mounted this wait-and-see attitude toward the whole thing."

When we last spoke in October 2001, Eric was still trying to day trade. For sure, he didn't have any regrets about giving up the law career or the long hours at the law firm. He did make some significant changes to his day trading business, however.

He was working out of his house instead of at the day trading firm and was spending less and less time pursuing his dream. He tried to take a more efficient approach to trading by monitoring profits and losses much more closely. Now if he feels something is not working, he turns the computer off and does something else instead of sitting in front of the screen all day losing money.

Peter Maestro owns a very successful family business in New York's garment center. His family on both sides are "garmentos" and have been for generations. Peter joined the family business right after college and took over for his grandfather when he died. He and his uncle own and run one business, while his father owns and runs another. The businesses complement each other, making for a good flow of referrals and opportunities for both companies.

Working in a family business is difficult and can often be extremely stressful and maddening. Those who have never experienced it have no idea what it is like and most likely cannot appreciate the freedom that comes from not working with or for your family. Still, it can also be very profitable and fun and, for most, the good times outweigh the bad.

For Peter this was not the case. His uncle was driving him crazy, and he thought it was time for a change. Yet the garment industry was all he knew, and he could not picture himself doing anything else.

His solution came from his friend Danny Clement. Danny suggested that Peter come work for him. Danny was a day trader at a firm in New Jersey. Peter knew Danny was doing great and began to think seriously about the job. After all, he had been trading some technology stocks and had made a good bit of money. He thought that if he focused on it all the time he would be even more successful.

Little by little, he began to learn more and more about how Danny traded and how the business worked. He found out that Danny had five other traders working for him who were also doing well. Danny's business was a little different from Eric's, because Danny funded the five people who worked for him and in turn kept a piece of the profits (the traders absorbed the losses completely). Eric worked for himself and did not share his profits with anyone, but he, too, had to absorb all of his losses.

Peter and I often have lunch together. Once we get through the pleasantries, our talk always turns to my questioning him about his business and his always asking me about the markets and various stocks that he likes at the moment.

Peter is a pure example of the people I described in the beginning of the book who believe that picking stocks is something everyone can do and that you don't need any training to be successful. He believes that he knows just as much as anyone else when it comes to picking stocks, regardless of the fact that he has spent his career working in the garment center. It is funny, because he would probably immediately criticize anyone who thought that they could succeed in his business because they know all about clothes (they've been wearing them all their lives).

When he first told me of his idea of becoming a day trader, I laughed. I could not believe he was willing to throw away a perfectly good business to go sit in front of a computer screen.

"It makes a lot of sense," he maintained. "The place is near my house, the hours are good, and I can make a fortune."

I tried to talk him out of it, saying that he was foolish, but he would not budge. I tried to tell him that the situation would have been completely different if he had just recently finished school and did not have a wife, two kids, a mortgage, and car payments. I strongly argued against his making the move.

In the end, he stayed at the family business. While I like to think that it was something I said, in reality I know it was the following story that caused him to be thankful that he did not pursue day trading.

When the market began to sell off, Danny was caught like everybody else. As his losses started to mount, he had to stop funding the five people who were working for him, and he began to have problems at home as well. No longer was he able to generate any profits, because the spreads had narrowed; and then when the exchanges moved to decimalization it was like a double whammy. Not only was he experiencing a bear market, but he also had to deal with pennies instead of eighths and quarters. Sure, the losses were not as drastic, because the stocks moved in smaller increments; but the gains were smaller as well.

Danny ended up losing all his trading capital. In the end, he decided that the only thing he and his wife could do was to sell their house and move into an apartment. When he told his wife that he thought it would be good if she got a job, she decided that the marriage really wasn't working anymore.

They sold their house and split up. She moved back to live with her parents, and he moved into the basement of Peter's house.

"It really turned out to be a nightmare," Peter said. "I can only imagine what it would have been like had I done it."

This is just one example of an extreme situation. Most day traders don't lose their houses or wives over their losses, but it can be very stressful and sometimes can push things to such extremes. There are a lot of once-high-flying day traders in Manhattan who are now waiters and waitresses.

If you ever wondered why the Dutch fell as hard as they did for the tulip mania, all you had to do was walk the streets of any town in the United States during the most recent bull market for a taste of the madness.

Ira is married and the father of three grown children. For more than 40 years he has owned a small retail business in a small city in New England. During the most recent bull market he made quite of bit of money (on paper) buying Cisco, CMGI, Amazon, and Netscape stock. Boy, the bug bit him hard. When the markets started to fall, he did not get out. Instead he doubled up on a lot of positions, which have continued to decline in value. Yet he remains hopeful that eventually the stocks he has will be worth something more than the paper they are printed on.

"I know the stocks will come back. I just have to wait for them to rally, and when they do I will be all right," he said.

Good luck, Ira.

This is what the markets do to people during the bull market and during its savage decline. The market gives and it takes away. Remember that the trader who does not have any money put away on the side will never live to trade another day!

The profiles in the previous chapters illustrate that hard work and patience are the keys to successful money management.

While everyone knows that patience is a virtue, most of the people who got into the market in the second half of the 1990s really seemed to lack it. They wanted it here and now, like everything else they believe they are due in life.

Investors need to keep in mind the old saying "Good things come to those who wait." Those who do will most likely be happier and end up with much more profitable trades.

Peter York and his wife Eve were married in 1975. Throughout their lives, he and his wife have both worked hard; they raised a family and basically lived the American dream. They reside in a very nice house in New Jersey (it's paid for), raised a couple of beautiful kids, and have some grandkids; basically, things are good.

Peter, a newspaper professional, was let go after 25 years at one company. For the next 10 years or so he sort of bounced around from paper to paper, finding work at one place or another for a few years, then going on to someplace else, and finally landing a job at a prominent financial news web site. After working there for about two years, he was downsized out of the job, and at this writing was still looking for work.

I was speaking to him in early October about the usual things that good friends talk about, and for some reason we started talking about his financial situation. He told me that two things saved him. First, he was able to buy quite a bit of Tribune Company stock at a discount while he worked there, and that continues to be a significant resource during his unemployment. What has helped him even more, though, has been a gift from his father-in-law on his wedding day: 50 shares of Johnson & Johnson. Now, 26 years later, it has grown to 1,800 shares worth almost $100,000.

"I really didn't do anything when I got the gift. I knew it was a good stock. People were still buying Band-Aids and Tylenol; J&J was introducing successful new products all the time. So I just let it ride, reinvested the dividends, and watched it split," he said. "Over time it has grown, and now that I am 63, it is worth quite a bit of money."

Peter's patience paid off. Sure, there are people saying that he probably could have made more or done better selling the shares and doing something else with the money, but in the end letting it ride worked out just fine. Most other investors will have the same success, as long as they find good companies with good products and managements who know what they're doing. It is work; it is not easy; it can often be frustrating and dull. But it is the way to go.

If investors do not believe in or are unwilling to practice the money management strategies outlined in this book, then in my opinion they should not put money in the market at all.

Remember that there is no luck in investing; there is only hard work.

GLOSSARY

accredited investor An investor who meets the Securities and Exchange Commission guidelines required for investing in hedge funds.

arbitrage A financial transaction involving simultaneous purchase in one market and the sale in a different market.

ask price The price at which the market maker offers to sell stock to a buyer; also known as the offer price.

asset allocation The systematic and thoughtful placement of investment dollars into various investments; such as stocks, bonds, real estate, insurance, and cash as well as a portfolio of mutual funds that include various investment styles, strategies, and focus.

balance sheet A constantly changing report of a company's financial positions that lists all of its assets, liabilities, and stockholders' equity.

bear market Prolonged period of falling prices.

beta The relative volatility of a particular stock relative to the overall market as measured by the Standard & Poor's 500

Index. If a stock's beta coefficient is 1, it means that its price rises and falls in direct relationship to the movement of the index. A beta of less than 1 indicates a stock that is less volatile than the overall market, a beta greater than 1 indicates that the stock is more volatile.

bid price For stocks it is the price at which the market maker offers to buy the stock from a seller; for mutual funds it is the net asset value.

book value The value of a company that remains if all of the assets were liquidated at the values carried on the balance sheet and then all liabilities are paid off. Intangible assets such as goodwill, patents, and copyrights are excluded from total assets.

broker A registered representative who acts as intermediary in the purchase and sale of securities.

bull market Prolonged period of rising prices.

capital appreciation An increase in the market value of a security or the overall market.

capital stock Amount of money or property contributed by stockholders to be used as the financial foundation for the corporation. It includes all classes of common and preferred stock.

capitalization Market capitalization is the total market value of a company's issued and outstanding shares.

closed end fund Mutual fund with a fixed amount of shares and assets. Its shares trade like a stock on an exchange, and the assets of the fund grow only through investment appreciation.

day trade A trade that is liquidated on the same day it is initiated.

derivatives Securities which take its values from another security.

due diligence Questions by investors to the manger regarding investment style and strategy as well as the manager's background and track record.

earnings per share (EPS) A company's total after-tax profits divided by the number of common shares outstanding.

Federal Reserve Board The governing arm of the Federal Reserve System, which seeks to regulate the economy through the implementation of monetary policy.

fundamental analysis The use of economic and business data to determine price.

leverage Means of enhancing return or value without increasing investment. Buying securities on margin is an example of leverage.

liquidity The degree to which a position is available in the market.

load Sales charge paid by an investor who buys shares in a load mutual fund—typically—5¾ percent of invested funds. Loads are usually charged when the investment is made; however, some funds charge a load for withdrawals, and this is called a back-end load.

load fund A mutual fund sold with a sales charge by a brokerage firm or investment professional.

long position A transaction to purchase shares of a stock resulting in net positive position.

management fee Fee paid to manager for day-to-day operation of the investment vehicle.

margin call Demand that an investor deposit enough money or securities to bring a margin account up to the minimum maintenance requirements.

mutual fund A regulated investment company that raises money from shareholders and invests in stocks, bond, options or money market instruments.

net asset value (NAV) An accounting term similar in meaning to book value or net worth; used as a reference to the value of a mutual fund.

no-load fund A mutual fund offered directly by the investment company to shareholders without a sales fee or commission. The funds are usually sold directly by the fund company rather through investment professionals.

open-end fund Mutual fund with an unlimited number of shares. Its assets grow through both investment appreciation and new assets.

performance fee Fee paid to a manager based on how well the investment strategy performs.

portfolio diversification theory The theory assumes that investors want the least possible dispersion of returns for a given level of gain.

price-to-earnings ratio (P/E) The price of a stock divided by the company's annual earnings.

quantitative analysis Security analysis that uses objective statistical information to determine when to buy and sell securities.

Sharpe ratio The ratio of return above the minimum acceptable return divided by the standard deviation. It provides information of the return per unit of dispersion risk.

short position A transaction to sell shares of stock that the investor does not own.

standard deviation A measure of the dispersion of a group of numerical values from the mean. It is calculated by taking the differences between each number in the group and the arithmetic average, squaring them to give the variance, summing them, and taking the square root.

12b-1 fee The promotional fees charged by a mutual fund, usually a no-load fund. The fee is generally 1 percent and by regulation must be disclosed.

volatility The degree of fluctuation over a given period in a security based on the standard deviation of the price.

volume The total number of shares traded during a given period.

NOTES

chapter one *Investing 101*

1. Friedman, Jack P. *Dictionary of Business Terms*. 3d ed. Hauppauge, NY: Barron's Educational Series, Inc., 2000, p. 119.
2. Ibid., p. 526.
3. Yue, Lorene. "Stock Market History: A Primer." *Detroit Free Press*, February 7, 2001.
4. Nasdaq.com. "Market Characteristics Section," August 27, 2001 (www.nasdaq.com). The data and research source was as of December 31, 2000.
5. Clash, James M., Lenzer, Robert, and Maiello, Michael. "The $500 Billion Hedge Fund Folly." *Forbes*, August 6, 2001: 70–75.
6. Benjamin Graham and David L. Dodd wrote the landmark book *Security Analysis* that laid the foundation for fundamental stock analysis. The book, which was first published in 1934, is considered by most to be the source for understanding how to look at companies and value their stock.

7. Lenzer, Robert, and Fondiller, David S. "The Not So Silent Partner." *Forbes*, January 1996: 78.
8. Ibid.
9. Loomis, Carol J. "The Value Machine: Warren Buffett's Berkshire Hathaway Is on a Buying Binge. You Were Expecting Stocks?" *Fortune*, February 2001: 70.
10. Ibid.
11. Lowenstein, Roger. "Graham and Dodd and Dow 6000." *Wall Street Journal*, October 17, 1996: C1.

chapter two *Growth and Value Managers*

1. Bloom, Ray. "Caution Is the Watchword in Investing; Main Question Is What Are You Looking For from Your Money?" *Detroit News*, May 8, 2001.
2. Morningstar, Inc. "Manager Experience Pays, Says Morningstar Study." PR Newswire, May 4, 2001.
3. Institutional Investors for the most part use managers to find firms for them to invest in; the consultants play a role similar to the one a retail stockbroker does with an individual investor.

chapter three *Sector Fund Managers*

1. Hakin, Danny, and Fabrikant, Geraldine. "Hedge Funds That Excel (and Avoid the Exotic)." *New York Times*, February 18, 2001: 1.

INDEX

INDEX

INDEX

INDEX